Bewbush Playbus

Dedication

I could not have said it better than the words of thanks from
Philip Avery on departing the Playbus.

**'To all those involved with the Bewbush Playbus.
With many thanks…
To the committee for all their hard work;
To the staff for their kind support;
To the parents for their loyalty;
To the children for their love and kisses;'**

**Whatever happens,
Keep it going'**

Hopefully this book will do that in spirit.

First published in Great Britain in 2012 by The Derby Books Publishing Company Limited,
3 The Parker Centre, Derby, DE21 4SZ.

© Sue Wickstead, 2012

ISBN 978-1-7809-119-84

SUE WICKSTEAD

Bewbush Playbus

Contents

Acknowledgements

The photographs within this book were collected from various sources; they have been gathered together as recollections of events in the history of the project.

The photographs were used in public exhibitions both nationally as well as locally. They were used to promote and publicise the work undertaken by the project.

At Annual General Meetings, training events and local venues, the aim of the exhibition was not only to highlight the work we did but to focus on the potential a mobile project could offer within the community.

The further aim was to not only thank those who had supported the Playbus but also to encourage interest and funding from a variety of sources in order to continue to operate as well as develop the project further.

As part of the National Playbus Association (now Working on Wheels) our project was seen and used further afield than just Crawley, it was involved in training events and government legislation changes.

In 1999 the *Times Educational Supplement* also took an interest, and our project was nationally recognised in an article written in the March edition. See page 189.

The Bewbush Playbus was a self-funded project which relied on its income from session fees as well as fund-raising. Although widely publicised and complimented on the work we undertook, the much needed funding did not materialise until too late. The project came to an end in 2003 due to mechanical difficulties in the bus itself. However, the fond memories live on for those who used or knew about us.

For further information on The National Playbus Association now Working on Wheels visit: www.workingonwheels.org.

Author's Note

I had for a long time, intended to put together the Bewbush Playbus information into a book, however, teaching commitments did not allow me the time to do so.

Following the untimely death of Angela Flatt, in 2007, who was a long standing supporter and Playbus staff member, it gave me the incentive to start to put the information together.

My departure from my role as a full-time teacher meant that now was the time to stop talking about it and get the job done.

There may be gaps missing or important photographs lost, but now it is done.

This is in memory of Angela Flatt and is dedicated to all those ever involved in this unique project.

Philip Avery

Philip Avery, the first Playbus co-ordinator /driver, said ' I have fond memories of 14 years of my life spent on this pioneering project.

'I recall the following personnel as being the ground workers of the project. The lynchpin was June Spaull of Crawley Social Services Dept. [the then under-fives' advisor for Crawley]. June was the first to get the project moving.

'Dave and Vic Hastings were members of the steering committee along with many others. The first playgroup supervisors were Barbara Conley, Sue Boxall and Lyn Constable, ably assisted by Angela Flatt and a small band of volunteers. During my involvement with the Playbus, a steep learning curve presented itself. Driving lessons from Syd Peters and tuition on starting portable generators, firing up the central heating and servicing chemical toilets, all had to be mastered.

'To say that you never know quite what will happen when you join a new project is for me a huge under-statement. How could I ever know that I would meet my lovely wife Val on a double-decker bus. (Val was the afternoon supervisor).

'Our wedding day was made complete by the appearance of the Playbus outside the church, and we rode as passengers to our reception. We found two bottles of champagne in the sand tray, which made the journey all the more enjoyable..

'Working with such a good team of staff and volunteers was wonderful, and the experience of meeting and working with so many Bewbush families and sharing their lives was a real privilege for me.

Philip and Val now provide foster care for special needs children.

What is a Playbus?

The beginning

Most people when you mention Playbus recall the 1963 British musical feature film *Summer Holiday* which starred Sir Cliff Richard. The story featured Dom (Cliff Richard) and his group of friends (Hayes, Green and Bulloch) who are bus mechanics at the huge London Transport overhaul works in Aldenham, Hertfordshire. During a miserably wet British summer lunch break, Dom arrives, having persuaded London Transport to lend him and his friends an AEC Regent 'RT' double decker bus. They convert this into a holiday caravan, which they drive across Europe, intending to get to the South of France. However, their eventual destination was Athens.

The musical film was a huge box office success which has now been produced as a stage musical in the West End. Although not anything to do with the Playbus movement, it did highlight the potential of using a double decker bus for purposes other than public transport.

The First Playmobile

Since the Plowden Report of 1967, the concept of Educational Priority Areas (EPA) had been widely discussed. One such place was an area of Liverpool which was once prosperous.

Following expansion of the port and its adjacent commercial life the area had seen a tremendous change in social living. With large rises in population it was over populated with high unemployment figures and much of the area was then standing empty with boarded windows, it had now become a target for vandals.

Dr Eric Midwinter, was appointed director of the Liverpool EPA project. The project was to look at what could be done both inside and outside school to offer an education that is community-based and socially relevant. The project's impact on children, teachers, parents and administrators indicated the wide-ranging possibilities of community education. The project was to focus on Education in Primary and Secondary as well as Pre-school and Adult education.

The pre-school campaign was aimed at extending provision in the area, the project had recognised that among the casualties of slum living are the very youngest children, there were few areas where small children could play safely and very few playgroups. With only one in seven or eight places available to the three to five-year-old age group this was considered an urgent area of development. The project began by looking at supporting site based pre-school groups but this proved disappointing. The business of taking children to and from playgroups, for a mother of a large family, could be an exhausting affair. A mobile solution was considered as a means of helping both children and their mothers in a more direct way.

The first ever mobile project, the Playmobile, was a pensioned-off bus bought in 1969 from the Liverpool Corporation which further helped to garage, service and fuel the project. It served the area of Paddington within Liverpool, which was considered an educational priority area.

The pupils from the local Comprehensive School became involved, supervised by the technical and art staff. They undertook the task as a piece of community service, painting the exterior and interior as well as undertaking internal conversion work. The interior had fitted flooring; dummy steering wheels; rope ladders; safety doors; table top desks and even a slide made from a plank and a converted oil drum. The conversion experience gave hands on practical learning to the boys involved, in both woodwork and metalwork as well as general maintenance.

The project relied on volunteer drivers who then drove and operated the Playmobile at three identified sites each week where it could offer a safe play environment. Many enthusiasts trying to start playgroups in this sort of area found that enthusiasm evaporated before they could raise the necessary support for a hall and enough funds to get the project off the ground. The Playmobile was designed to assist such a situation, by setting up and establishing a group it could therefore move into a more permanent location. The Playmobile could then move on to help set up other groups within a community.

Apart from practical difficulties like drivers falling ill, lack of staffing and so on, one of the more pleasant problems was the possessiveness of groups. The Playmobile could not only give support to the groups but could also act as an advertisement for custom, the sight of a huge, brightly coloured bus in the back streets of Liverpool brought plenty of mothers and children running. The Playmobile made an impact wherever it toured focussing attention and the groups were loathe to see it move on.

The publicity generated in press and television coverage and stimulating interest in the EPA project work, and specifically in pre-school provision, was inestimable. The Playmobile had shown that its flexibility could help meet the varied and swiftly changing patterns of pre-school needs.

The Next Step

In 1970 this idea was copied, the Ealing Playmobile in London was the first, followed quickly by one in Sheffield and Bristol. Rochdale had one planned and Coventry also had a Playmobile in mind for its Hillfields area. Ulster had five, three in Belfast and two in Londonderry. The Playmobile also helped to present 'nursery for all' petitions to Westminster. The idea of using old buses to provide community services began to spread. The Playbus was a highly visible resource which could reach out to isolated and deprived areas moving in and out as necessary.

By 1973 there were so many Playbuses that it was recognised that a National Organisation needed to be set up to represent the interests of the mobile community work. The National Playbus Association was constituted and run by dedicated volunteers from member Playbus projects from around the UK. It was able to further offer advice, support, training and networking opportunities to its members.

In 1977 a number of projects, including Bewbush, received funding and support as a result of the Queen's Silver Jubilee Community funding.

In 1978 the Department of Health agreed to fund the National Playbus Association in recognition of its work in supporting the voluntary sector as well as the Scottish Office for work in Scotland. This funding helped many

At the Newcastle Rally 'National Flower Festival'

small organisations, Bewbush among them, to apply to the NPA for funding purposes as well as support and advice.

By 1980 the membership had grown enormously and each of the regions now had their own sub-divisions networking within their own areas. Of these some of the most active were SCAMP (Scottish Association of Mobile Projects); SWAMP (South West Association of Mobile Projects); LASER (London and South East Region). Each of the regions worked to inform their members and campaign on such issues as changes in the under five's working laws as well as EU Driver Legislation. They were also accountable and working on behalf of the National Playbus Association based in Bristol.

So what is a Playbus?

A Playbus is a bus used for providing mobile facilities for a variety of activities surrounding entertainment and education. Although it conjures up images of under eight's play, in fact, mobile work covers a wide variety of services and support.

The typical UK Playbus is a double decker, retired from active service, converted from passenger carrying into an equipped space suitable for children's play activities. It will have a heating system, power supply (often separate or on-board generator), kitchen, storage space, toilet (portaloo).

The interior is made to welcome children, as well as practical for staff and volunteers. The exterior is decorated with bright eye catching designs to reflect its use and clientele, which gives a colourful impact. On board safety features include fire extinguishers as well as fire escape routes from the top deck.

However, since early pioneering days mobile projects have made many more technological advances in both space and design as well as types of vehicles now deployed.

Playbuses have been used in a variety of play settings: including under-fives work, many as playgroup and Parent and Toddler bases, sometimes free standing and sometimes linked to an existing fixed site provision such as a play centre or community centre.

They have also been used to work with school age children in after school and playschemes context, providing service to communities where nothing else has been developed or to enhance and support work already in existence.

However, the potential and use of a mobile is far more.

Playbuses are 'community buildings on wheels'. They offer venues, staff and services to communities where there are not enough community buildings to provide the necessary services, where there are obstacles or funding problems to address.

They are able to move in and support a need being self contained and flexible. A Playbus or mobile community vehicle in any form can operate as:

A crèche
Pre-school or Parent and Toddler group
Playgroup
Twilight youth drop in
Outreach or detached youth centre
Advice and information centre
Toy library
IT centre
Holiday play centre
Training/advice centre
Environmental education centre
Mobile sensory centre for disabled children and adults
Health advice centre
Mobile arts/DT centre
Mobile gym
Mobile cinema
Mobile library
Promotional tour bus
Political battle-bus

Mobile projects form a unique contribution within community and their value and potential is endless. They can, and do, serve communities where there is no alternative, but a mobile project can be a highly visible resource deployed into an area to help provide a need, serve a community and pave the way for permanent provision.

Advantages of mobile work

They are highly visible and attractive not only to young children but to the community.

They are flexible and can move in to support an area of need for development.

They are adaptable and mobile.

They are self-contained and well equipped for the service required.

They instil a sense of ownership not only from the staff and volunteers but the community they serve.

Disadvantages of mobile work:
Finding a safe site to operate can be difficult.
They can be cold in the winter and hot in the summer.
They can be temperamental and at times difficult to maintain and service.
Finding a safe place to park up away from vandalism can be awkward.

But all in all any mobile project is not like any you have seen before. As its doors swing open it becomes a magic kingdom full of enticing nooks and crannies for any age person. It is a place to meet, greet and explore, is cosy and self-contained.

For many of those who have worked on, or with, a mobile projects it becomes an enthusiastic love unlike any other project. It is this ownership and passion that keeps many projects active and working beyond many difficulties and promoting mobile work. There are many mobile projects, although not always now part of the one membership group, yet the possibilities are endless.

National Playbus Association
The National Playbus Association has now changed its working title to Working on Wheels. At the start, a Playbus was exactly that, a converted second hand bus kitted out to provide play opportunities for young children in deprived, mainly urban communities. Now forty years on the membership provides much more: services to communities in cities, towns and villages throughout the UK, in specially converted vehicles ranging from buses, trucks, trailers and vans of all shapes and sizes. The new working title reflects the wide variety of projects and uses.

Working on Wheels serves to provide vital information and support services which help keep its members on the road and assist new projects through their setting up stage: these include information and advice helpline, technical advice, designing new vehicles, vehicle safety checks, affordable motor and liability insurance, training conferences and workshops, promoting good practice and safe operating standards. It also offers networking opportunities to meet other mobile users formally or informally. Keeping its members informed about mobile work, new legislation, government initiatives and ideas through regular newsletters and update mailings.

For further information on Working on Wheels visit:
www.workinghonwheels.org.

At the Newcastle Rally 'National Flower Festival' Howgill Hippopotabus (BBC's Challenge Anneka Project).

Harlow Rainbow bus

'Sparky' Glasgow Bus.

Exeter 'Bizzybus'

Toybus

Playmate

Creche Mobile

Bristol Playbus

Supersonic Playbus Bewbush

The Bewbush Playbus was one of the many community projects started as part of Her Majesty's Silver Jubilee celebrations.

In 1977 Her Majesty the Queen celebrated 25 years as reigning monarch and many organisations were invited to raise funds to support community projects. In view of the amount of money collected by the Girl Guides Association, for the Queen's Silver Jubilee, they were allowed to choose an area to help. Supported by grants from the Queen's Silver Jubilee Fund and the Department of Education and Science the scheme was to encourage and train its members in Community Leadership.

The Girl Guides South-East Region chose to serve the new area of Bewbush, Crawley, West Sussex. The area of Bewbush was then a new and developing district within the New Town of Crawley. Crawley Borough Council could not, at that time, afford to build a much-needed community centre. The area was still expanding and was also without a definite centre or even community school for the young children.

A committee was set up and included members from within the area of Bewbush as well as representatives from Social Services, the Girl Guides and the local church. It was decided that a community bus would best suit the need as it would be mobile and could move as the area expanded. The committee, in conjunction with British Caledonian Airways and The British Airports Authority, were able to provide a bus. The bus was meant to fill a temporary gap and could move to other areas as the need required.

June Spaull of Social Services remembers originally purchasing the vehicle, from Eastbourne Corporation, for £300 with a further £400 to buy the tyres. Appeals were then put out in the local press asking for help to refurbish the vehicle for use. Following negotiations with nearby Gatwick Airport arrangements were made for the bus to be converted. The bus was completely stripped and refurbished and painted inside and out by British Caledonian.

The original paintwork design had a Girl Guide figure in detail to reflect their involvement in the project.

ALL SYSTEMS
GO FOR THE
BEWBUSH
BUS!

The Supersonic Playbus. Doesn't
it look great fun?

The work of the Girl Guides was a feature in their 1980 Annual.

British Caledonian Airways also agreed to undertake the conversion work as well as the exterior paintwork. This was paid for by British Caledonian and British Airports Authority. BAA additionally paid for the first years running costs.

The committee and children arrived at the British Caledonian aircraft hanger to take ownership of their newly converted Playbus. Now painted, converted and ready for use. They were able to present a framed letter of thanks to those from the airport who had helped this happen.

Christopher and Daniel Hastings are seen presenting a framed letter of thanks to British Airports Authority and British Caledonian.
Dave Hastings, Pat Bailey (BAA Airport director), Steve Martin (Church Army), Mrs E. Burbridge (Girl Guides commissioner), Bill Richardson (Engineering director for British Caledonian Airways).

On behalf of the children of Crawley who will obtain pleasure and benefit from the Supersonic Playbus.

I would like to thank the management of British Airports Authority for its generous help and expertise without which the Supersonic Playbus venture would not have been possible.

It is appropriate that in Gatwick's 50th Anniversary Year this successful and worthwhile community project should reflect Gatwick's success and local importance.

This Supersonic Playbus will never leave the ground but in the imaginations of many happy children a flight in the Supersonic Playbus will be an adventure.

Yours Faithfully.

S. Martin

Chairman.
Bewbush Playbus Assoc.

Presentation letter which was presented to both BAA and British Caledonian. One of the original copies was returned to the Association by Pat Bailey of British Airports Authority many years later. (While at school one day Mr Neil Pelham, one of the original committee, was pleased to see it back with the Association history and proudly informed me that he had written both the originals in calligraphy.)

The New Supersonic Playbus flew to Bewbush where it parked up and was used for a Summer Play scheme.

Inside the top deck of the bus, which was used for quiet Art and Craft activities.

The fire exit slide leading from the top deck of the bus was always a favourite, allowing the children to sit on the bonnet.

Later modifications and alterations extended the length of the slide and adding stairs made this a popular piece of play equipment for the groups.

On behalf of the children of Crawley who will obtain pleasure and benefit from the Supersonic Playbus.

I would like to thank the management of British Airports Authority for its generosity help and expertise without which the supersonic Playbus venture would not have been possible.

It is appropriate that in Gatwick's 50th Anniversary Year this successful and worthwhile community project should reflect Gatwick's success and local importance.

The supersonic Playbus will never leave the ground but in the imagination of many happy children a flight in the supersonic Playbus will be an adventure.

Yours Faithfully

S. Martin

Chairman
Bewbush Playbus Association

From then on the 'Supersonic Bus' was used as a play centre for the under fives. It contained among other things, a kitchen, a painting and sand play area, a playhouse and was decorated outside in a brightly coloured aviation theme.

The brightly decorated Playbus operated from the district of Bewbush, here it is seen situated at the side of the Bewbush Leisure Centre.

Social Services remained involved supporting the project over the years and were able to find and provide a driver worker, Mr Philip Avery. The playgroup was able in return to provide spaces for those children and families, referred to by Social Services as needing support.

Lady Baden-Powell handed the bus to the community of Bewbush, in August 1980.

Silver Jubilee Plaque

*The Queen's Silver Jubilee Trust award for service to the community was
presented by Lady Baden Powell to the Bewbush Playbus association.
It was not possible to display the award on the project itself due to vandalism
and was placed in safe keeping for display purposes.
The Plaque was returned to the committee in 1990 and was put on
display for our projects history exhibition which was used to further
highlight our work and help with fund-raising efforts.*

The children through our doors

Playgroup

In 1980 when the Playbus was given to the area of Bewbush there was at that time no shops, school, community centre, or leisure centre.

Initially the bus was used as a summer playscheme. However, with so many young families in the area there was a great need for pre-school play provision.

The playgroup was set up and supported by Social Services who at that time provided a driver worker for the project. The bus initially would drive back to Gatwick Airport in order to park safely overnight.

The bus would park up during the day where it could and invited children to experience art craft and play opportunities. The parents became the

1982 Morning Playgroup

1982 Afternoon Playgroup

committee and were then responsible for the day to day running of the group. Mr Bill Dempsey, then manager of the Bewbush Leisure Centre and parent, gave the project the permission to park up safely beside the Leisure Centre. This offered a safe and static site to operate from as well as help saving funds from fuel and maintenance.

Inside the bus the atmosphere was calm and relaxed. Its low roof, condensation covered windows and the warmth from flickering gas heaters created a cosy environment where workers and children played together without the usual din associated with under fives.

The Playgroup was registered to offer a maximum of 16 places for children per session with three staff on hand.

Both the morning and afternoon groups were well attended and supported. The morning group, run by Sue Boxall and Lynn Constable, was open for five mornings

1983 Morning Playgroup

1983 Afternoon Playgroup

while the afternoon group, with Val Wiseman as supervisor, was available on three afternoons.

Parents and helpers were encouraged to support the project however they could by offering help with fund-raising, bus maintenance or support within the group sessions.

1984 Morning Playgroup

The playgroup continued to be in high demand with a long waiting list. Due to this children would be offered two sessions initially either in the morning or the afternoon, which would be increased to three as available once they were four years old.

The intention was that as the area of Bewbush grew the bus would move to new locations as needed. However, with the large number of young families with young children in the area the demand for spaces remained high, despite now

1984 Afternoon Playgroup

1985 Morning Playgroup

an adventure playground, community centre and cricket pavilion also offering pre-school places.

As the area grew the bus moved and the bus became a familiar sight at Bewbush Leisure Centre, where it provided hours of fun for under fives and a welcome break for young mums and dads. The Bewbush Leisure Centre

1985 Afternoon Playgroup

1986 Morning Playgroup

provided a static stable site from where the bus could operate safely. It also had facilities for the bus to fill its water tank and plug into an electrical power supply.

In 1987 the old bus was given new life with its new livery painted by Gatwick Engineering.

1987 Morning Playgroup

1987 Afternoon Playgroup

The Nursery Rhyme theme supported our under fives work with many familiar rhymes on display. The Playbus this year proudly led the Crawley Carnival procession.

1988 Morning Playgroup

1988 Afternoon Playgroup

However, with the now aging bus becoming more unmanageable it was decided to raise funds to buy and replace our existing project. This was a tall order but very necessary as demand for pre-school places was still very much in demand.

With additional pre-schools opening in the area the playgroup decided to become a morning only group, allowing the bus project to extend its mobile

1990 Morning Playgroup

Children waving from the top deck windows of their new red bus.

work to incorporate alternative session work. This included both Rising 5's and Parent and Toddler groups in Bewbush as well as Ifield Hyde Drive.

Our new Red Leyland Atleantean arrived in 1990 and was then ready for mobile use by the many groups, events and activities it could offer. However, the new bus needed further modifications and changes to the conversion so at this time both buses were in use.

'It may be cold in winter and hot in summer, cramped and unreliable but if you're eight years old or younger, a multi-coloured double-decker bus full of noise and children takes a lot of beating as a wonder of the world.'

Playgroup picture but no bus.

Inside the Playgroup

Adults in the area were invited to register their children onto the playgroup waiting list. Each playgroup session was offered for a two and a half hour duration with both a morning as well as an afternoon group on offer as and when places became available. At the age of three children could be offered two sessions either morning or afternoon which could then be increased to three when the children were four years old. Despite other playgroups in the area the demand for spaces meant there was always a full waiting list. Session fees were necessary to pay staff wages as well as buy materials and equipment. All other funds were undertaken by both staff and management committee at events etc.

Inside the Playbus the children were able to explore and play in a safe and welcoming environment. The cosy atmosphere created a calm place with art and crafts as well as play opportunities.

The water tray cover doubles up as a craft area. Here Rebecca McPhereson, Jack Keeling and Dipesh Nayee are busy sticking their pictures in place which are then hung up to dry ready to take home.

On the lower deck of the Playbus children could paint, draw or play in the sandpit. Jack is creating his artistic painting, while Adam is playing in the sandpit. Joanne Voss and Tina White are busy with their drawings. Katie Lawrence is just having a 'miss my mum' moment with reassurances from me.

Outside play equipment, including the trampoline, needed to be stored wherever there was a space, ready for outside summer play.

The lower deck was for all the messy craft activities as well as a sand play area. It also had the kitchen with counter space as well as the porta loo toilet. Both decks had a heating gas system which added to the cosy warm feeling inside. The water tank was filled from the tap nearby at the leisure centre. The bus was compact and well equipped ready to cope with any session, storage of the many resources was located in any small nook or cranny

On the upper deck of the Playbus Philip Avery watches on as Dipesh Nayee carefully builds his brick wall. Jack and Adam are ready to step in as necessary.

Lee Cooper sits on the stairs unsure of whether to go up or down.

that the bus could offer. Paints were mixed daily and it was always a sure favourite with the children. Over the painting area was a line where the masterpieces were hung up to dry ready to take home at the end of a session.

The upper play area offered a cosy calm environment where the children could play safely with the toys, play in the Wendy House, or quietly read books. The toys were stored in under-seat storage areas or in a cupboard at the top of the stairs.

Elly Riddick has arrived on the top deck ready to play.

The upper deck of the Playbus had a curved surface, the road playmate could be laid out, here Eleanor and Tom Riddick, Daniel Hale and Matthew Morris are enjoying playing with the cars.

During any session children were able to move freely between activities and areas as they felt. The stairs might be steep but because the children knew they were they took care when moving between decks.

At the back of the bus children enjoyed playing in the beautiful 'Rose Cottage' playhouse. Inside the playhouse there was a play kitchen area as well as fancy dress storage. Also there was a secret trap door which was the fire exit. From here the children were lowered onto the bonnet of the bus and slid down the slide.

Fire drills were carried out each term and provided a happy play opportunity for the children to play on the slide unaware of the important role that the slide played. The slide had to be out at every booking and when waiting for the group to open the children could climb the steps onto the bonnet and play on the slide. This was always a favourite with the children.

At the end of the playgroup session children would tidy away the toys and the downstairs area was cleaned ready for the next session. The children would then sit and have a drink and biscuit ending the session with songs or a story then wait ready to be picked up by their parents.

Sitting on the bonnet press newspaper photo.

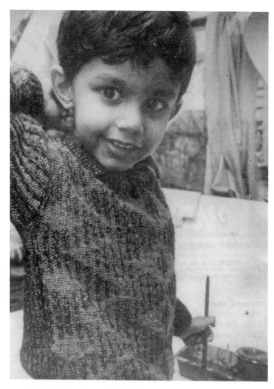

Dipesh Nayee

Helper Philip Avery

The new livery

By 1986, when my son joined the Playgroup, the beautiful decoration on the side of the bus had not only faded but had been subjected to attacks of vandalism and graffiti. The name 'supersonic' had been painted over in an attempt to sell advertising space. It was definitely beginning to show its age.

The heavy mechanical steering of the bus made it more and more unmanageable to drive for our volunteer drivers who were prepared to take it out. It was further suffering from mechanical problems and was starting to break down and become unreliable. Its replacement parts were now museum pieces and not only expensive but difficult to find.

The committee of volunteers relied on support from its many users. Without the bus the playgroup could not continue and once again the committee made a plea for help.

It was at this time I offered to help on the committee and as an art teacher, offered to look at repainting the Playbus. I set about looking into this and

The original 'Supersonic' seen parked at the Leisure centre in Bewbush.

spent much time while my son was in the playgroup sessions, looking into designing and drawing plans to repaint the bus.

Thinking of the project as a playgroup for under fives I looked into designs on a nursery rhyme theme and made an appeal for books to help with this.

It was Angela Flatt, a parent and registrations secretary, who came up armed with books to help and I then measured the panels of the bus and drew and painted full sized designs based on many favourite Nursery Rhymes. I spent the next few weeks drawing and painting the intended designs to scale, measuring the bus and location. Most of this work was undertaken during the two hour sessions that my son was at the playgroup with my young eight-month-old daughter sitting quietly watching.

By February the ideas were well under way and we were looking at possibly undertaking the painting itself during the Easter holidays when the playgroup would be closed. However, it was still a tall order and looked impossible.

It was suggested that we could get free paint from a Dulux Charity paint appeal and with this in mind I started to research the quantity of paint we might need. It was at that time that I got in touch with Gatwick Engineering to ask their advice as to how much paint we would need. Frank Holmwood's response was not to use Dulux paint as it was not the right type of paint for

The newly painted bus seen from the driver's side.

Bus now in location and once again ready for action.

the intended purpose. He listened as I explained that as a Charity we would have no option and then said he would look into Gatwick Engineering undertaking the work for us...free of charge.

It was agreed for the bus to be spray painted with the blue and green top and bottom. Over the next few days I took in the full sized picture plans and traced the sketches directly onto the bus for Mr Holmwood to paint the pictures. With one parent helper who started to paint the flowers along the bottom we watched as the designs took shape.

Little Boy Blue sleeps above the entrance door.

Humpty dumpty with a cheery smile!

Little Boy Blue slept over the door while Humpty Dumpty greeted the children from the doorway.

Miss Muffet frightened by the spider or the children on the exit slide?

Little Miss Muffett sat by the exit slide frightened by the spider. Meanwhile on the other side of the bus Little Bo Peep was looking for her sheep.

Little Bo Peep still can't find her sheep!

The illustrations were all for the traditional Nursery Rhymes that the children sang in playgroup. We should maybe have looked at updating these or thinking of making the illustrations more multi-cultural in design but the traditional designs seemed more appealing. With hindsight the designs made the project very young but, in fact, all ages recognised the Rhymes and all ages appreciated the simplicity as well as the cheerful aspect it gave to the bus itself.

Jack and Jill tumble down from the top of the bus!

Jill

The full sized designs helped when it came to adding the designs to the Playbus as they were used to trace the designs onto the now green and blue base colour. Additional details were added including the blue hot air balloon which held the Girl Guide logo and also the signpost pointing to Holmwood.

Jack

The old woman who lived in a shoe? Or is it a bus?

The Old Woman's Shoe was placed above the driver's cab door. Maybe not a shoe but in the Playbus she certainly has many children to entertain.

Baa Baa Black Sheep was another favourite.

Baa Baa Black Sheep

Two Little Dickie Birds sitting on the wall beside Humpty's welcoming greeting.

Later on after its return we painted the Nursery Rhyme *Hickory Dickory Dock* on the inside of the door. The clock door would open on time for the group sessions.

On the wall beside Humpty we had placed Two Little Dickie Birds, while Humpty sat close by hand held to indicate Gatwick Engineering's Logo.

We discovered during one summer, when the doors were open and tied back, that Humpty ended up looking through the toilet window! His big eyes peering in! Naughty Humpty.

All in all the result was that we now had a beautifully painted and restored project which we could proudly take to events. But I apologise, I did not know that the bus was called 'Supersonic' and belonged to Crawley and not just Bewbush. The name 'Supersonic' had been painted over so when it was repainted it was named 'Bewbush Playbus' and with its now young Nursery Rhyme livery it might have suited the younger user but did limit our image and we would need to enlighten people as to how a mobile project could do much more than work with under fives only.

Playgroup parties & events

Christmas party 1987

With all the efforts put into fund-raising, for a Gala day and Santas grotto, the management committee decided to say thank you to the parents and children for their support and efforts. We wanted to give something back to the playgroup so we decided to hire a magician for the children's Christmas party. We hired the Waterfield Adventure playground for the occasion.

Uncle Hughie entertains the troupes.

Uncle Hughie gets the children involved.

Excited children were able to gently touch and see the birds and animals from Uncle Hughie's act.

We booked Uncle Hughie the Magic Mystic. He performed various tricks and even got some assistants to help him. The party was provided for both the morning and afternoon bus playgroups. The children had come in party clothes and had made special party hats for the occasion.

Uncle Hughie delighted his captive audience of three and four year olds, who sat attentively and patiently throughout. He let the children see and gently touch the small animals and birds from his magic act.

With curiosity they saw the tame birds close up and gently touch.

First the Conga.

After the magic act came the dancing and the party games; both morning and afternoon playgroups joined in together.

Next the children, now tired out, sat down to enjoy a picnic lunch.

Then the Hokey-cokey.

Sitting down on the floor the children enjoyed a picnic lunch.

Finally while singing Christmas songs for the mums and dads Father Christmas arrived with a sack full of presents. After giving a toy to each child the party was over and the children left happily for home.

Tom Riddick receives a present from Santa.

Maxine and Elly enjoy the bouncy soft play.

Playgroup summer trip 1990

In 1990 at the end of another very busy year fund-raising the playgroup booked a summer trip to Brighton where they would visit Pirates Deep. The children travelled by coach and then had the opportunity to explore and experience the inside activities assisted and supported by the ever-present playgroup staff.

The children had the chance to race around in safety and were excited by all the possibilities to explore and investigate their space. But just in case the playgroup staff were ever watchful and present reassuring any who were more hesitant or unsure.

Philip Avery – playgroup Social services support worker – reassures those who are a bit hesitant.

The children explored the hidey holes.

The children found places to hide and play happily where they could let their imagination take their ideas and develop.

The children were already used to the cosy contained bus environment but this was full of soft play and ball ponds.

Soft play house

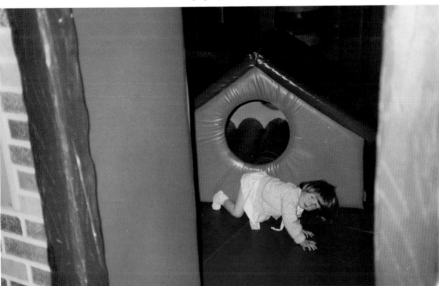

In the ball pond.

The children loved to be able to immerse themselves and swim in the ball pond and loved burying themselves underneath the plastic balls.

Burying themselves in the ball pond.

Lunch was eaten in the café.

Onto the beach

After all the hectic and exciting fun the children adjourned to the café area to eat their packed lunch.

After lunch we had enough time to visit the local beach and to run over the pebbles gathering shells and watching the waves. The Playbus staff were on hand to ensure safety. Then at the end of the day we gathered together making sure we were ready for the trip home after all the excitement.

Ready for home

Crawley Carnivals

1987 – 'Pantomime'

The Crawley Carnival held once a year in May, gave the opportunity, driver allowing, for the Playbus to join the fun. If there were volunteers available the bus could further undertake fund-raising activities by opening its door to the many visitors.

In 1987 our newly painted Playbus led the procession. The theme for this year's carnival was Pantomime, although we would have liked to do *Peter Pan* it seemed appropriate to keep the pantomime in keeping with the new paintwork. So we opted for the Nursery Rhyme *Mother Goose*.

The front of the bus now clearly said who we were! 'The Bewbush Playbus!' We had also added a further note explaining that the project had been started with the Girls Guides for the Queen's Silver Jubilee Celebration. The two jolly Bewbush trees were the logo used in Bewbush both in the First School as well as on the front of the Leisure Centre.

The Playbus was invited to lead the procession.

The starting point for the procession was at the bus station and we led the way through the town and along the High Street to the carnival ground in West Green. No we did not knock the traffic light down!

The children in the Playgroup were invited to join in the fun and to come in fancy dress. As it would be too far to walk a carnival float was organised and the children were able to ride to the carnival ground on the back of the trailer.

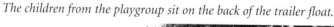

The children from the playgroup sit on the back of the trailer float.

Parents sit with their children safely.

Parents could come along with their children and once on the field would wander off to visit the fair. This year the weather was not too wet so the bus was able to park safely at the side of the field.

The children had been able to sit safely on the float and even had their lunch on the long journey around the carnival route.

Elly Riddick eating her lunch   *Tom Riddick float*

The bus parked up and if parents were available, could open up to allow children to play inside or experience the exit slide route.

Driving through the streets of Crawley the bus then drove onto the field where this year the children were invited to pay a penny to go up inside the Playbus and then out through the emergency hatch and down the slide. Always a favourite!

In addition the bus was a good focal point for any lost children at the carnival.

Once onto the field both my son and daughter were entered into the individual fancy dress costume competition. Tom won the first prize as a Hot Cross bun seller while Elly as Miss Muffett tried to steal his buns!

Tom Hot Cross bun seller

Fancy dress competition

Philip Avery and his wife Val, formerly Val Wiseman, came along to support the newly painted bus. Val had been playgroup afternoon supervisor and met

The fancy dress competition took place in the main arena.

Philip and Val

Philip Avery, from Social Services, while working together in afternoon playgroup sessions. Philip was also working in the morning playgroup for four of the five sessions, his role was further to be available, offering advice and support to the management committee.

1988 – 'The Wild West'

In 1988 The Wild West was the theme and we even made our own banner this year. 'Cowboys and Indians, we all play together on the Playbus.' We had organised the procession so that the children could ride on the bus if they got tired. Despite it being a long walk the children and adults preferred to walk proudly ahead of our Playbus.

Again once onto the field we took the children to the individual fancy dress competition. Tom and Elly won the first prize as card shark and saloon girl, and Joseph Gorman third prize as a gunslinger.

We had made a banner using our new logo.

Group in front of the bus ready to lead off.

Group workers with children in tow.

It was a long walk but we preferred to walk rather than ride.

Black and white picture shows fancy dress winners, with first and third place going to the Playbus playgroup.

1989 – 'The Circus'

In 1989 the theme for the carnival was The Circus. Our old bus was now breaking down and temperamental, we did not think it would last the procession. Fortunately we had just received a grant for £5,000 from West

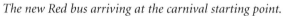

The new Red bus arriving at the carnival starting point.

Sussex County Council and had been offered a bus for that amount from Gatwick Engineering.

So here it is our new red bus!
The bus was not decorated so my brother David walked down to the local supermarket where he picked up lots of large cardboard boxes. He then cut out the letters for our name and got the local children in the street to paint the letters.

It was a quick and impromptu playscheme. The letters were attached to the side of the bus with tape. But on arrival at the meeting place car park the 'E' had dropped off so we had to quickly make another one. Good job the bus was so well equipped!

The small children arrived in

We quickly needed to make another 'E'.

Group shot at the door of the bus

their fancy dress: Clowns; tightrope walkers; jugglers; Lions and lion tamers, we all joined in! Some of the costumes came from the bus collection and some were expertly made by our parents.

The bus, as always, was the focal meeting point.

Joseph Gorman came as a cheery lion while his brother Barry looked great as a clown.

As always it was a lot of fun and a lovely sunny day. Fancy dress costumes would

Joseph and Barry Gorman

Geoff in hat

then be added to the Playbus collection.

Whole families could join in with dads as drivers. This year it was my husband, Geoff Riddick, who offered to drive the bus. He even managed to put on a hat for the occasion!

The bus won second prize and was given a cheque for £10 for the playgroup.

1990 – 'Cartoon'
In 1990 the Playbus organisation was contacted last minute to help with children's entertainments at Gatwick Airport. The flights were being delayed and we were asked to help relieve the boredom for the children stuck in the queues to get off the ground. As the project was undertaking much needed fund-raising activities it was seen as a good way to not only raise necessary funding but also to provide work experience opportunities for our many volunteers. We agree as long as we could make the carnival procession for the playgroup. While operating at the airport the young visitors were encouraged to draw pictures which were then used to decorate the Playbus exterior.

The red bus with pictures attached.

The Playbus was very well received by the many visitors at the airport and following many complimentary messages the bus was further booked throughout the school holiday months. It gave the bus a real chance to increase its funding but also to serve a wider audience.

We all gathered together for a group shot.

1991 – 'As seen on TV'

In 1991 with the carnival theme As seen on TV the Playbus had to go as *Playbus* (later changed to *Playdays*), which was a TV programme for under fives and featuring a Playbus that visited many stops including Peggy Patch stop and the Why Bird stop.

Now with new groups operating on the bus, in particular the After School Group, it brought in more support as well as older school aged children joining in the fun. Big brothers and sisters, whole families joined once again.

The children's costumes were bright, cheery and colourful which matched the sunny day. Some of the costumes were from the bus but many were made by the parents and could then be added to the fancy dress collection on the bus itself, such as traffic lights and lollipop men with banners.

Richie Matthews looked great dressed as Why Bird.

Walking together in the procession with our bus following.

Front of bus with Tom Riddick, Elly Riddick and Gemma Rigby.

Group waiting patiently at the front of the bus.

Children of all ages joined in the fun – adults too! With photographs taken by Julia's husband, Jon Rigby, we certainly had a great record of this carnival. But we had earned the attention!

The black and white shot of Elly Riddick and Richie Matthews appeared in the local paper.

Black and white procession shot.

Elly Riddick with bus stop sign.

Having now been given the use of a spare classroom in the First School it gave the opportunity for the bus stop resources to go up on display within the school. As well as start the Playbus exhibition.

Euro Tunnel Tom and Elly Riddick.

1992 – 'Into Europe'

Crawley Carnival 1992, we must have forgotten our cameras this year as there is only the one photograph as evidence and it is not at all clear what the theme was. It was something to do with going into Europe hence the Euro tunnel link.

1993 – 'Pantomime'

1993 the theme for the carnival was again Pantomime. In 1987 when the theme had also been pantomime we had considered doing *Peter Pan* but as the old bus had just been painted we had matched the theme to Nursery Rhyme so now it seemed appropriate to do *Peter Pan*.

With lots of different groups now using the bus, each one was enlisted to help in some way.

The group poses at the side of the bus.

Murphy mob! A whole family gets involved!

I had, at this time, joined the local school's teaching team and made links through this association to encourage support from the wider community for the bus rather than the playgroup only.

The after school group made lost children tags and Playbus slogans. The playgroup made pirate faces for the windows while my class at school helped make Indian faces as well as headdresses and pasta necklaces.

Our chairman, Gary Murphy, as driver was forced against his wishes, to wear the crocodile hat and stop watch we had made him. He enjoyed it really but would never admit it. Anyway he made a good crocodile – not too snappy!

Gary Murphy – driver and part time crocodile!

But Paul Murphy certainly stole the show and looked the part. Dressed in his red coat and wig he made a very convincing Hook! He certainly entered into the spirit and frightened many a child on the way round the procession.

Everyone had put a lot of effort into their costumes especially the Parent and Toddler groups who came with mermaids in buggies and vehicles to match the pirate theme.

Standing, at the entrance to the bus, ready to greet those who came along.

Paul Murphy dressed as 'Captain Hook'. A scary sight

As usual we preferred to lead the Playbus and walk the long procession.

It had been a lot of effort but we once again won the first prize for the second year running. Yet another event full of fun and hard work but we could now march happily through the procession looking forward to next year.

Leading the procession from The Hawth theatre car park.

The windows of the bus had our own rewritten nursery rhyme on display.

1994 – 'Nursery Rhyme'

1994 and this year the theme of the carnival was Nursery Rhyme. With memories of the old Playbus we rewrote all the favourite nursery rhymes first featured on the old bus, giving them all a Playbus slant.

There was an old woman, who worked on a bus,
She had so many children who made such a fuss;
So she gave them some paint and she gave them some glue;
And she showed them so many things they could do!
And they are happy now!!

We had invited all of our many groups to get involved and undertook artwork in each group to support this. We had offered some of our fancy dress costumes to the children but as ever they came up with their own wonderful ideas.

Paul Murphy, one of our group workers, was persuaded to dress up once again. This time he dressed as the old lady who lived in a shoe, or in this instance the old lady who lived on the bus. He did say he did not like dressing up, but we think he was fibbing because he really did get into the part.

Paul Murphy with his son Darrren and Michael Flatt. The children were very taken and in awe of Paul and his many dressing up disguises!

Group poses together at the side of the bus.

Geoff Riddick: Jester Driver.

We persuaded Geoff Riddick, this year's driver, to dress up. He was 'Jester Driver'!

Paul Murphy: The Old Woman, with Sue Wickstead: Little Miss Muffett.

Holly Lucas came as The Queen of Hearts, while Alice Elliott looked sweet as Mary Mary Quite Contrary.

Angela Flatt: Wee Willie Winkie.

Incey Wincy Spider – Eleanor Riddick sits in the middle of the group shot.

But the bus could not be complete without Humpty Dumpty himself! So we made a large papier-mache Humpty to sit on the back fire exit of the bus, on his wall.

Humpty Dumpty thought he was cool.
Humpty Dumpty felt such a fool.
He'd used all the paint
And he'd used all the glue
Now Humpty Dumpty had nothing to do!

We had put up the old photographs of our original Playbus with nursery rhymes and once again the bus came first in its category.

Humpty on the back of the bus.

Back of the bus shot. With Michael Gunningham and Carlie Murphy.

1996 – '50 years of Crawley'

We did not take part in the procession in 1995. The Playbus had finally been sponsored and paid to attend as an attraction, which was now held at Southgate Playing field. Although the carnival was a lot of effort, it was also felt to be an important date in our calendar. It was good for our funding to provide entertainment, but somehow this year we had felt something was missing. As we watched from the field as the procession arrived we felt we had lost out and missed the fun.

It looked like 1996 would be the same. We had been offered a float and it was suggested we work together with the newly formed 'Bewbush Happy Hut' who provided after school care, to enter the procession.

However, the staff and committee agreed we wanted the bus to go into the procession and then to work on the field as an attraction afterwards.

The theme this year was 50 years of Crawley. This was a tricky one, but we finally looked at the town's development and picked a building theme.

The groups designed and made house pictures to reflect the districts of the town: collages, drawn, painted.

Michael Gunningham, Katie Hardwick, Eleanor Riddick and Sharon Hardwick:
Bewbush Happy Hut Crew.

Each of the groups were invited to attend and came dressed as builders and workmen with tools to hand.

Once again the Murphy mob and friends.

John Kearns – from the Happy Hut group and Ryan Murphy from the Playbus Playgroup joining forces.

The numbers were small but those who did attend made a lot of effort. Individual fancy dress prizes went to some of the playgroup children with the Happy Hut winning second prize in the under 12s category.

The weather held off until the procession, which was just enough time for the bus to not only win in its category, but also overall in the carnival cup.

We didn't make it onto the field as the weather and ground conditions were so bad but at least we were there and were able to show that we were very much part of Crawley and its history.

This was the last Crawley Carnival held in the town.

Elly Riddick and Katie Harwick second prize winners in the under 12s group.

Katie Harwick with Emily Knipe from the Parent and Toddler group.

Michael Gunningham ready with his town architect plans.

The new bus

Although the playgroup had become a successful and popular use for the bus there were a few committee members, mainly dads, who saw the potential of the vehicle itself.

Once we had a beautiful attractive Playbus again, adorned with eye-catching paintwork, it was decided that we should set our sights towards the possibility of replacing it before it was too late.

The bus was now in a poor mechanical condition narrowly passing its MOT test. Spare and replacement parts were now difficult to find, expensive and museum pieces. The bus became mechanically difficult and unreliable to drive and would constantly break down. Although there was no danger to the playgroup and other users, the difficulty in finding volunteers prepared to drive such a heavy unmanageable vehicle, put the whole mobile project at risk.

The Playbus had found a static site to operate from and rarely moved, this was fine for the playgroup but not for the potential of the project.

The Association decided that it would set its sights on a new bus and to raise funds however, and wherever it could. To this end the project sought to attend fund-raising events, with or without the bus, as volunteers were able. It was a tall order given that we all had small children in tow but it was considered necessary in order to continue our work.

We also looked into further possible uses for the bus when not in use by the playgroup: these included a Rising 5s group, after school group, playschemes, as well as bookings at events – we even rented out the bus for children's parties. Apart from the events most of these uses relied on the vehicle operating from its static site due to lack of drivers and the unreliability of the vehicle.

Ariel photograph taken in @ 1990.

With new residential dwellings being built in the area of Bewbush, the need for playgroup spaces would remain for a further 10 years at least, with no alternative site available. It was therefore considered a priority to keep the well-

Our new red bus had arrived and was now ready for action.

The red Bus decorated with bunting and balloons.

Lady Mayor, Councillor Brenda Smith cuts the ribbon officially opening the new bus.

loved bus in operation and our appeal was launched to buy and convert a suitable replacement before it was too late.

Further to this the committee visited other local bus projects to gain ideas as to additional uses and conversion layout.

The appeal took over two years of hard concentrated work. We managed, at last, to raise necessary funding for the new bus. The bus was used by our playgroup for its summer trip to The Bluebell Railway thanks to one of our dads, Trevor Bastin, who held a PSV licence.

However, although we were thrilled we also knew that there was still so much more to do to convert the vehicle itself for group use. We continued with our fund-raising and sought advice from NPA. The bus itself was much more visible and this did help us in our grant applications and requests. This proved that we were not only determined but serious in our quest.

The conversion work was then secured and under way in Kent but finally in 1990 we saw the arrival of the newly converted Red Leyland Atlantean Bus. Our Energy Bus – registration number NRG 176M.

The Playbus was suitable decorated with bunting and balloons ready for its grand opening. The Playbus Exhibition was on view for everyone to read.

The new bus was now officially opened in June 1990 by the then Lady

Mayor, Councillor Brenda Smith. We had decked our bus with bunting, organised a fund-raising event and invited not only our members but interested parties to come and see our project. As well as view our photographic exhibition on display.

The new semi-automatic bus was much easier to drive and many of our members and workers were happy to do so.

The association not only came to realise that a mobile project could do so much more but also saw the potential. The bus was not only able now to continue to serve the under fives but was also able to extend its services to incorporate Parent and Toddler, Rising 5s, after school clubs, mobile play schemes, youth work, support work for the airports delayed passengers and many more nurture groups planned or being considered. But most of all we knew we could achieve much of this because our bus was much easier to drive and we were more confident we would arrive at our given location easier.

Photograph has Brenda Smith with, myself, Sue Wickstead and some of the playgroup children. Barry Gorman, Carlie Murphy, Richie Matthews, Alice Elliott, Holly Squires, Nikki Jones, Katherine Ellis.

The way ahead, dressing up

We began our new bus fund-raising campaign by holding jumble sales as often as we could. We would load the bus with the sorted jumble and take it to the venue.

Through parent contacts at the airport we were lucky to be donated some 'salvage luggage' which we collected in the bus from the airport and sorted through. Some items went to the jumble, some we were able to add and make up tombolas and raffle prises.

Role play and dressing up has always played an important part, not just at carnival time but also in the groups. Some of our mums offered to use the clothes from our many jumble sales to make fancy dress costumes for the children which was always a favourite with any group.

Send in the clowns

On parade – our fighting force

'Evening all'

'Best of friends'

'Fly me to the moon!'

'I'm so tired today!'

'I demand to see the captain!'

'Yes madam?'

'Tea up!'

'We have waitresses at our restaurant…'

'*…and chefs!*'

The staff joined in the fun dressing up too. As part of our fund-raising we came up with the idea of collecting donations direct from the public. Having gained permission from various venues around the town we dressed up as clowns and arrived with collecting tins in hand. In answer to any questions as to 'what is a Playbus?' we could point and say 'there it is outside and ready to take us on to the next venue'. It was a fun event which brought a lot of laughs but also relied on a suitable driver.

Our first event, 'Clowns', proved so popular that it was repeated with 'Blues Brothers' and 'Pirates'.

Jumble sales were a good start but a lot of effort so we had to think of new and exciting ways in which to raise money. As ever it relied on our fabulous parents and volunteers.

Clowns at the ready

Sponsored Events

Our parents and volunteers also helped where they could with sponsored events included London Marathon, sponsored slim, sponsored bike ride.

On different occasions the children in the playgroup helped to raise money for both bus repairs and new books by collecting a yoghurt pot full of change. The children were given a certificate or had their names put into the books with a dedication plate.

Yoghurt pot pennies to collect for books.

Crawley to Brighton bike ride.

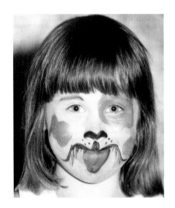

Face Painting

At one of the training sessions we attended, members of staff learnt the skill of face-painting and with professional paint this was not only a success with the children, but also the staff. It also led to us being able to support other groups including summer schemes and school fairs adding not only to our fund raising but also as an additional attraction and resource.

Carlie Murphy with her face painted as a puppy dog.

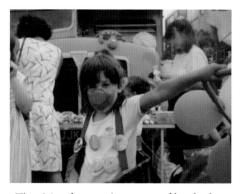

Tina Murphy wearing many of her badges.

Badges

Another good fund-raising activity we were able to invest in was a badge machine. The badge making was offered to the other organisations and charities with us supplying identity badges for other groups including the Archery Society as well as fund-raising for Comic Relief.

Events

In addition we tried to improve our local image and attended as many fund-raising and public events as we could, not only the carnival but also:

Crawley High Street Fair
Goffs Park Fun Day
school fairs
 Hawth Theatre Happy Days
British Airports (BCal) Wellie Olympics
Santas Grotto

We were even acknowledged in the Crawley Fair publicity advertisement.

Picture of Margaret Murphy at a local event beside the bus fund-raising.

Art work picture

At many of these events we raised much needed funds from voluntary efforts: selling refreshments, promotions, organising tombolas, as well as opening up the bus as a play area. We were able to buy many new toys and resources for the bus groups, primarily the playgroup, as well as put money aside for maintenance of the vehicle and additionally the new bus fund.

At these events we would also spend as much time as we could talking to the public about our work and telling them of our fund-raising target, not knowing who we would be talking to or how they could help or could offer. This was made very clear to us after a very long day fund-raising at the Crawley Fair. We had talked to anyone who had shown an interest. Angela Flatt remembered talking at length to an elderly couple who seemed interested in our plight. Some weeks later, out of the blue, we received a cheque for £100. It had been Lord and Lady Longley that Angela had spoken to and they had made the donation from the Longley Trust Fund. It was a welcome donation and quite unexpected.

During this time the bus began to show its age and broke down on many an occasion. We once had secured a place at a Christmas Fair in town where the bus would attend and open up as Santa's Grotto. We had spent a lot of time and energy decorating the interior of the bus and had Santa ready standing nearby only to find that the bus would really not move at all! Not only did it break down but had only managed to move 100 yards then spluttered to a stop. Fortunately it was still in a safe location for the group to operate but we had to find the funds to sort it out and move it back. All this cost the Association unnecessary worry and expense from a fund we were trying to build upon. This did take its toll on our fund-raising efforts but we still managed to battle on.

This sad event did draw in interest from the local press and the local free paper *Newsbreak* came and produced a wonderful article on the project. The article had a series of black and white photographs, taken by Jon Rigby. This further highlighted who we were and what the project did.

It became apparent to us that the Playbus was perceived to have a limited use and range of services. With its livery of very young art work and the fact that it operated solely in Bewbush as a playgroup facility, then its value would also be limited. Why should it receive support?

Exhibition

Following the publication of the article in *Newsbreak* paper we decided that it was now a good time to not only publicise our work further but to improve our profile image.

We got in touch with the Social Services who, with June Spaull, had been very much involved in the beginning of the project. Social Services had continued to support and assist the project by supplying a driver worker, Phillip Avery, who worked in the playgroup. Without this support the playgroup could not have financially survived. It was limited by numbers it could offer playgroup spaces to and therefore wages and costs would have been tight. Despite the project no longer being mobile at this time the support had been continued and Philip undertook many important tasks regarding maintenance and safety aspects on the Playbus itself. From here we also managed to get a brief history of the start of the project.

Following this we spoke to the Girl Guides Association to find out more. We also found an article on the start of the project in the 1980 Girl Guides Annual. We also discovered that we had been awarded a solid metal plaque from Her Majesty the Queen's Silver Jubilee Community Awards scheme. Unfortunately, due to threats of vandalism, the plaque had never been able to be displayed but could now go into our exhibition.

Our campaign began to generate interest in the press and we appeared constantly in local papers as well as nationally in the *Times Education supplement*. Together with all the group photographs that we currently held we were able to put on exhibitions at both the Crawley Library as well as our AGM.

Our newly restored membership links with National Playbus led to us looking at ways to improve our current group services and looking at other uses for the Playbus.

Grants

We used the information gathered to support our search for funding from a variety of trusts and awards. Some of the successful applications provided new toys and equipment for the groups while others went into our core funding new bus appeal.

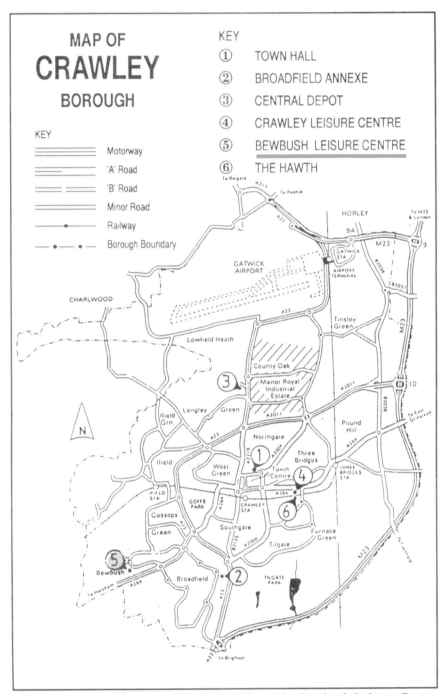

The Bewbush Playbus operates at the side of the Bewbush Leisure Centre

Map

LEYLAND ATLANTEAN NRG 176M

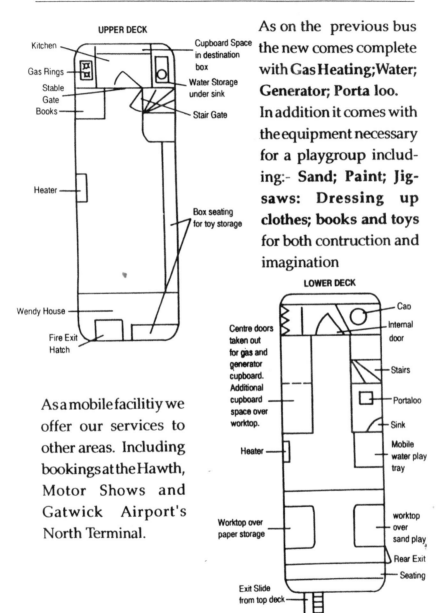

As on the previous bus the new comes complete with **Gas Heating; Water; Generator; Porta loo.** In addition it comes with the equipment necessary for a playgroup including:- **Sand; Paint; Jigsaws: Dressing up clothes; books and toys** for both contruction and imagination

UPPER DECK

Kitchen

Gas Rings

Stable Gate

Books

Heater

Wendy House

Fire Exit Hatch

Cupboard Space in destination box

Water Storage under sink

Stair Gate

Box seating for toy storage

As a mobile facilitiy we offer our services to other areas. Including bookings at the Hawth, Motor Shows and Gatwick Airport's North Terminal.

LOWER DECK

Cab

Internal door

Stairs

Portaloo

Sink

Mobile water play tray

worktop over sand play

Rear Exit

Seating

Centre doors taken out for gas and generator cupboard. Additional cupboard space over worktop.

Heater

Worktop over paper storage

Exit Slide from top deck

Inside bus layout

Logo

At this time we also came up with our own bus logo which we had put on T-shirts to sell to our user clients as well as for our workers to wear at fund-raising events to help identify who we were. This logo was then put onto badges, key rings, letter headed paper, posters as well as any other communication and promotion that we could come up with. We worked alongside the Playbus at events wherever we could. This not only gave us shelter but with our own kitchen area we were very self-contained. The only event we did turn up to without the Playbus was the market charity stall and we all agreed it was much easier to answer questions about us when we had the project behind us.

In 1990 and 1991 the project paid for a publicity booklet to further highlight ourselves and the work we undertook. It was seen as a valuable fundraising tool promoting further our forward momentum. The back cover showed a map of Crawley on which key locations in the town were highlighted and in particular the Bewbush Leisure Centre (Number 5) where the bus operated. While inside, the bus layout was added.

Playbus helps out at Gatwick Airport

The old bus outside the North Terminal.

In 1990 the Bewbush Playbus Association had been contacted by Gatwick Airport Ltd to ask if it could help in any way to help keep children occupied as an industrial dispute was about to commence. This was seen as a great fund-raising opportunity and the Playbus went to park at the North Terminal where it offered a quiet haven for children (and adults) caught in the delay. The bus parked near to the terminal where children could visit for any length of time free of charge.

The association with the airport led to further bookings during other school holidays. At first the old bus attended and with commercial fees charged the proceeds went towards paying and training staff as well as into the much needed fund-raising for a new bus. It also gave the project a safe place to park over the weekend away from the now unwelcome attacks of vandalism. The bus would drive to the airport and park on either the paved area or nearby grass area to offer its services.

New bus at the North Terminal.

Both buses on a field area at the airport.

Parked up ready for action on the nearby grassed area.

The new bus with its new livery.

The work at the airport not only enabled us to buy, convert and paint the new bus but also gave us necessary funding for equipment as well as subsidising our group development work. Our work also led to negotiations with Gatwick Airport Limited and British Airways asking them to help us out yet again. As they had both been involved in the initial start of the original project this was seen as a good community link with the airport.

Gatwick Airport Limited agreed to pay for the new livery while British Airways agreed to undertake the painting in their aircraft hanger. By chance we found a sign writer, Karen Boswell Studio 33, who could help out with designing the illustrations and Gatwick Airport also agreed to pay for them to undertake the sign writing designs.

We had organised the painting so that the project could take our newly painted Playbus the many miles to Newcastle upon Tyne where, at Gateshead, it would join the procession of Playbuses through the town as well as attend the National Playbus Training Event this year.

The equipment was transferred between each vehicle and the new, mobile bus, left the old bus to entertain at the airport, while it travelled the 10 hour journey to the training event in Newcastle.

The new bus just painted was shiny and presentable. We were proud to show it off at the Gateshead publicity event where so many other mobiles were also on display. Here we met up with a variety of projects from all over the country, including projects which had been helped by the *Challenge Anneka* BBC television programme.

The paintwork was completed just in time and the weekend before the two Playbuses were seen at the North Terminal where the old bus took over the duties of the new bus.

The livery of the new bus linked the blue and green of the old bus as well as images to reflect the links with the airport. With the British Airways Jumbo Jet on one side pulling the 'Playbus' banner and Gary Gatwick tows the banner on the reverse side.

The young girl reading her Playbus book to Gary and Gloria Gatwick is supposed to be my daughter Eleanor.

The new bus entrance side

The new bus drivers side.

Gloria Gatwick waves off Gary in his plane while our logo red bus travels over the bridge at Waterfield's Ifield, Mill Pond.

Both Gary and Gloria Gatwick Bears were given to the Association for any young child who may be in distress due to delays as well as used in fund-raising raffles and tombolas. They were a favourite in the soft toy box.

The back bumper of the bus had the Playbus name as well as Tweedle-Dum and Tweedle-Dee tumbling over as the bus moved on its journey.

Gloria and Gary Gatwick enjoying a cup of tea!

Tweedle-Dum and Tweedle-Dee tumbling about cheerfully!

Gary Gatwick in his plane.

BA jumbo jet.

Our links with the airport were reflected in the designs. Gary Gatwick flew in his plane on one side while the British airways aeroplane flew on the other side, both towing the bright 'Playbus' banner.

Above the door were the control tower and airport vehicles.

Above the rear window we had added the tree symbol for 'Bewbush', once seen at both the Leisure Centre as well as the First School Logo, another link

Flight control terminal and airport vehicles.

Both buses return to Bewbush now in matching livery colours.

with Bewbush as well as with the old bus. The name at the front and over the door now clearly read 'Bewbush Playbus – Crawley'. We felt despite our base in Bewbush we were part of the whole town.

Community Links

Over the years many of our children moved on from the pre-school playgroup to local schools and as such we made links through this within the local schools.

As we were seeking to extend our work and develop our project further we looked to use these links more constructively. We then started our first additional group the Rising 5s. At the time children did not get offered a space within school until the term of their fifth birthday which meant that we sometimes had children who were five or nearly five and these children seemed to want a little more than the playgroup session gave them. The Rising 5s group was started by myself with assistant, Sarah Damon, we offered spaces for 10 children who were four or more. The session still offered a play and craft session but this time there was a little more structure and direction. With only two staff it meant that the children stayed on whichever deck we were working on at the time and the structure was more in control. I had linked with my son's class teacher, Lorna Samways, from the local school to discuss what sort of things they would like the children to do. It was important that it was not seen as a teaching session but a group offering more directed learning through play.

The group continued to operate until schools began to take in Rising 5s into school by which time there was no longer the need for the group to operate.

Following on from this a meeting was set up to discuss our intended group development with Karen Lane, who was then Headteacher of Bewbush Community First School. One area we sought to develop would be a multi-cultural group.

Karen Lane was happy to write a letter of support for our work and following this we were given the use of an empty classroom in which we could set up an office base. This further enabled us to not only gather together information but help organise the display material which could be used in our promotion.

Schools Curriculum Award
1990

WEST SUSSEX COUNTY COUNCIL

BEWBUSH COUNTY FIRST SCHOOL

DORSTEN SQUARE, CRAWLEY, WEST SUSSEX, RH11 8XW

Headteacher: Karen Lane B.Ed., M.A.   *Telephone:* **CRAWLEY 517006**

29 April 1992

BEWBUSH COUNTY FIRST SCHOOL STATEMENT ON THE

FUTURE OF THE BEWBUSH PLAYBUS

Bewbush Playbus has provided an excellent service for young children in Bewbush. The Playbus is run by a highly motivated trained teacher - in terms of professionalism, commitment and vision.

Together we have recently been discussing plans for extending the educational role of the Playbus in the community. I was excited by Sue's proposals which include offering a peripatetic service to local schools. The playbus would be on site and its facilities, for example, would be used class by class on a rota basis or as a resource for children with specific needs.

Dependent upon adequate funding Sue's proposals for establishing a multi-cultural group (with clear short / long term aims and objectives already committed to paper) would provided a sound framework on which schools can build.

Bewbush Playbus must not only survive but grow, as is it an extremely valuable community resource. I have already declared my unwavering support to this end.

Karen Lane

KAREN LANE
Headteacher

Letter from Karen Lane

Bewbush County First School Statement on the

future of the Bewbush Playbus

Bewbush Playbus has provided an excellent service for young children in Bewbush. The Playbus is run by a highly motivated trained teacher – in terms of professionalism, commitment and vision.

Together we have recently been discussing plans for extending the educational role of the Playbus in the Community. I was excited by Sue's proposals which include offering a peripatetic service to schools. The Playbus would be on site and its facilities, for example, would be used class by class on a rota basis or as a resource for children with specific needs.

Dependent upon adequate funding Sue's proposals for establishing a multi-cultural group (with clear short/long term aims and objectives already committed to paper) would provide a sound framework on which schools can build.

Bewbush Playbus must not only survive but grow, as it is an extremely valuable community resource. I have already declared my unwavering support to this end.

Karen Lane
Headteacher

(Copy of letter written by Karen Lane and to be used to support our funding bids, dated 29 April 1992.)

In summer 1993 I was asked to cover a term teaching the Rising 5s, with schools now taking in the younger children the Rising 5s on the Playbus had served its purpose, and this was seen as a good opportunity to forge closer links. During the summer term it was agreed to bring the bus into the school grounds for the reception classes to experience.

Despite many children living in Bewbush, many had attended different playgroups and may not have seen the Playbus. The reception children made ribbon banners with our materials, collected from Merton Scrap Scheme.

Out in the playground they could play excitedly and, in small groups, were then allowed to experience the play inside the vehicle too.

The chance gave us the opportunity to promote the Playbus further but also to gain an idea into what the needs were and how we could support the community further.

In addition, the Rising 5s this year became involved in assisting the Playbus in getting itself ready for the forthcoming carnival by making Indian head dresses and decoration for the event. They were further invited to join us, or just come along and show support.

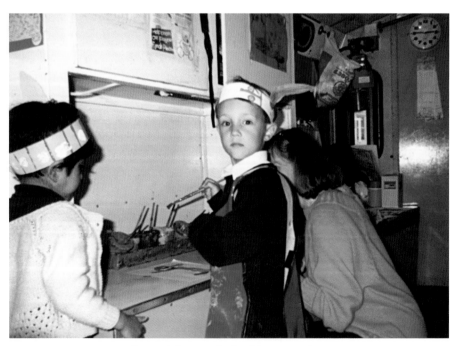

George Mason painting his masterpiece.

Ryan cook and Brett Daniels enjoying the play dough.

The Playbus coming into school was by way of a thank you for their efforts.

While some groups played outside. other children had the opportunity to go inside – on the lower deck they could paint a masterpiece, play with the play dough, or even play in the sand pit.

Meanwhile on the upper deck children had the chance to play with the brio train, dolls house; jigsaw puzzles or just read quietly. At least now the children knew what the inside of the Playbus held and were aware of what it was.

In the following year the After School Club was invited to move its group into the school grounds and in addition the Playbus offered the bus to the school to help with setting up a nurture group.

Further links with the community were forged when we helped to advise and inform the council in setting up a Scrap Scheme, where projects could access recyclable materials to use in project work. This was similar to a scheme we had also joined in Merton, which offered free recycled materials to voluntary projects. The items on offer included ribbon and soft play matting among other things, all helping us to offer more arts and crafts and reducing our material costs. Crawley Borough Council expressed an interest in setting up a similar scheme in Crawley, which now still operates from the Bewbush

Community Centre.

Together with the school we also helped set up a more permanent After School Provision in the local Community Centre. The Bewbush Happy Hut offered after school care for five evenings as well as summer sessions and in later years even a Breakfast Club. The Happy Hut offered play opportunity to older children leaving the bus to concentrate on those of first school years.

Playing in the sand pit

When the school reclaimed their classroom the Playbus Office moved in to share the Community Centre office with the Happy Hut.

The bus continued links with the school attending the summer fair and assisting with fund-raising both for Comic Relief as well as other events in the district of Bewbush.

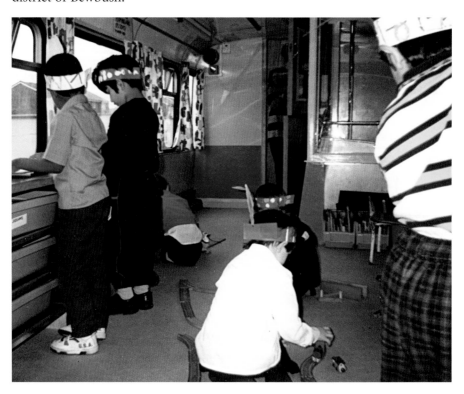

The children through our group doors

After School Club

Now we had a new reliable red Playbus, the project started looking at how it could extend and develop its project work. Although our playgroup was a secure and well attended group it was also seen to limit our profile and image. We needed to extend our groups to cater for older children. This would not only help with funding but also enable the bus to move on.

As many of our children were attending the local primary school we decided that we should look towards opening after school. We started with the one session on a Thursday with a view to opening more groups as and when funding would allow.

The After School group needed to cater not only for an older age range but needed to offer a safe outside environment for the children to play in safety.

The group with the totem pole.

The first group operated beside the Leisure Centre and we began to theme our activities.

One of our first groups undertook an Indian Wild West topic, where we could offer art and craft activities making head dresses and ethnic jewellery. As a group we put together an Indian totem pole and created our own face paint designs. Outside we added all aspects for our 'Pow Wow!' It was a lot of fun and another photographic opportunity for the local paper.

Tom, Ian and Elly suitably dressed as native American Indians. How!

During the winter months the group moved its location from beside the dark Leisure Centre and the group operated at the local shops car park where it ran with internal lights blazing. The group during the winter focussed more on playing games inside.

During the following summer the Playbus was offered the opportunity to open its group from inside the schools perimeter and the bus drove onto and parked on the school playground. This not only offered a connection with the school, making the bus more visible, but also gave the group a safe well contained outside area on which to play. During the summer the bus would move onto the field.

Inside the Playbus on a dark winters evening!

Group of boys standing by the rear of the bus.

John, delightful in red.

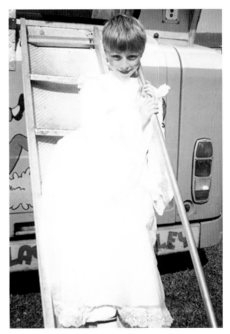

Graham in bridal dress.

Seamus Higgins stands on the slide.   *Group pose.*   *Graham and John pose for the camera.*

As ever one of the most popular activities was the dressing up clothes and children of all ages loved to create their own role play. At the beginning of one session some of the boys decided to dress each other up. I suppose they were expecting to be told off!

After the initial fun it was suggested that we could further use our face paints to keep them in role. The result was not only a lot of fun but gave a lot of very glamorous looking boys. They enjoyed posing for photos and took to their parts with enthusiasm.

Graham looked the part and loved his wedding dress. He looked beautiful, but John went more for the shy coy look.

Even Seamus 'dared' to join in. He even let us paint his face and posed for photographs. It was a lot of fun and well contained. Martin went as far as to dress up in a spacesuit. He didn't want the face paint but did join in the fun.

No one got too silly and most important of all was that the activity had been led, dictated and developed by the boys themselves.

Times Education Supplement article

During a difficult time in the school's history we managed to keep the After School Club going. We had joked that it was like a therapy session, but in fact it really was. The Thursday session on the Playbus enabled me to escape quickly from the school and gave us the adults the chance to play, talk and be with the children. For some children the group offered the same opportunities in their lives too. Some of our children attending were undergoing great changes in their own lives too and the bus offered a respite from their problematic lives. It offered a chance to talk, and to listen for both group staff as well as children. It worked both ways.

In 1999, the National Playbus Association was celebrating the 30th year since the first 'Playmobile' in Liverpool. Our After School Group was one of those featured in the *Times Educational Supplement* (*TES*). The article was about some of the after school group provision offered by Playbus projects. A professional photographer was sent by the *TES* to take photographs of

Theo Black in striking pose.

our group in action. Our group photograph was featured in the article as well as front cover of the NPA's magazine *Busfare*. In addition, the picture of Theo Black kicking the football was selected to be used nationally by the National Playbus Association, taking centre slot in their promotional display board.

Here Emma, Ruby and Alex are dressed and ready to enjoy their Chinese meal and social occasion.

Table ready

Tea party group

Role play and dressing up as ever a popular part of the upper decks enabled the children to enjoy the opportunity to play together in whatever role play session they chose to create.

The boxed seating stored equipment when not in use, at the side where further cupboards and shelves where equipment could be stored in trays and worked with on the table tops. The new bus upper deck had been converted leaving a level floor, something once suggested by Philip Avery.

Play together

Dressing up

The children could play quietly and safely and in comfort.

We did not have a Wendy house on this bus, it was an area we did look at developing, but never quite got round to it. The back window had a safety grill as it could be opened and dropped down for ventilation. The back of the bus held a fire exit trap door which dropped down onto the rear bonnet where children exit down a slide.

During the lighter summer months the session could operate more outside play opportunities and brought in equipment to suit the needs. The safety of the school grounds gave the group a secure play space free from other users and animals.

In the safety of the school grounds the children could use the wide open playground space and would use the outside equipment to further develop their imaginative ideas and just have fun playing in relative safety.

The outside area could be used to play with trucks.

The group continued to offer a drop-in session for children whose parents were working or who might otherwise be playing out on streets without supervision.

With changes in emphasis in literacy and numeracy within the school's curriculum play is an important part of a child's learning.

The Association invested in a wide range of outside play equipment some of which could be stored on the bus and brought out for use at whatever venue. The Quadro took a lot of initial construction work to put together but once built it could be part deconstructed and brought out each time. Yet small trucks and pull along toys proved just as popular. Much of the outside equipment was invaluable at the airport where the bus catered for a wide age and area of visitors who used the facilities for short or longer sessions of play.

One of the most popular pieces of equipment on the Playbus was the 'Fantasy Cube', which was a brown wooden box that hinged open to reveal cogs and dials and plug in attachments. In fact, it proved so popular with every age range that we eventually bought a second larger version. Closed, it was used as a seat or

The children loved the 'Fantacy Cube'.

a work top but open, it became whatever the children turned their imagination and role play to be.

Many of our fancy dress clothes came from donations but it was always the hats the children preferred.

But what is it about boys and dresses?

Dean and Gemma enjoy wearing their hats!

Christopher Dunning loved the pink dress.

The After School Group proved to be popular. However, we never did manage to open a second one. Some of this was due to timing, some to funding and staffing. The school moved into difficult times and our head teacher who had supported our work, left. The new head had to get the school out of Special Measures so the Playbus was not considered a priority. Sadly new construction and outside play area development for the Reception area within the school meant that access to the school grounds was no longer accessible. The group moved for a time to the leisure centre where it could use the park but it was no longer a sole user and the group eventually closed its doors in the hope it could move on to incorporate other areas of use.

Some of the playgroup children came back to work as volunteers within the group once they were older.

Group sitting on the Playbus stairs.

The after School group photographs were taken for the TES article 1999

Playschemes

With a fully working semi-automatic bus we were confident that we had a reliable mobile project to offer both Bewbush and Crawley. We had also been lucky to have a volunteer bus driver trainer who then kindly gave his time to take the many volunteer drivers out in the newer bus bringing our driving standards up to PSV standards. This was safer all around, not just to the project but also to the confidence of our staff and volunteer drivers. We looked into developing our image and reputation and set about forging links with other agencies including Crawley Borough council and Community Arts.

Following this we were booked to attend many events at the Hawth Theatre:

Hawth Happy Days

International Festival /Mela

Jazz Festival

Folk Festival

Children's Fun Days

It was also agreed that Community Arts would fund a play scheme which was to visit local neighbourhood shopping centres.

The idea was to visit as many sites as possible offering play opportunities to young visitors.

From here we would have a clearer idea of local needs, where the children were and would not only bring the project to a wider clientele but would help to identify areas which would benefit and respond from future support.

The first scheme was arranged for half term school holidays and the plan was to visit 10 different sites in a week. The two locations, morning and afternoon, would be closely located geographically. The bus was to open in the morning for two hours and then would move off to a new location for the afternoon.

Some children attended nearly every session while some came for only one. It proved not only a success for the Association but also to widen the perception that the Playbus only worked in Bewbush.

The face painting was always a favourite. This year the Teenage Mutant Ninja Turtles were a real favourite, many green faces were painted to the delight of our children if not the parents!

Elly Riddick

Mobile Playscheme group shot.

Elly Riddick as a Teenage Mutant Ninja Turtle at Southgate.

Following this, further schemes were organised and set up. This time we stayed within one area for both morning and afternoon sessions.

Social Services expressed an interest in the scheme and in return for specific areas they wanted us to support, they agreed to some part funding. The scheme was an overall success and was certainly seen as the right move in terms of our service provision.

In 1992 we were successful with a grant application from the BBC's Children in Need appeal and we looked into setting up and organising a four week scheme during the summer holidays. We were also at this time booked for the airport work as well as support for local play centres, Adventure Playgrounds and The Hawth Theatre Events. In addition, we were also asked to supply face painters for the Summer Scheme at the local Bewbush Leisure Centre. It looked like a busy summer ahead.

With further support and interest from both social Services as well as Crawley Borough Council we wanted to look at servicing as much of Crawley as possible in order to gather information on areas of potential needs and development. We looked into neighbourhood sites around Crawley locating as near to the centre parades as possible and with a safe grassy area for outside play. The outside area would be used to offer more range of activity in the summer months, including a bouncy castle and parachute for cooperative games.

We offered support in Southgate, Southgate West, Pound Hill, Ifield, Bewbush, Langley Green, Furnace Green, Three Bridges, Tilgate, Broadfield, Gossops Green and Ifield Hyde Drive. Some locations were well attended and others slower; weather and site location dictated the level of service we could offer.

On two occasions two of our parents organised their own scheme within their own house location. Maxine McPhereson chose to set her scheme in Brettingham Close, while Margaret Murphy used the Worthing bus on Saturday on a grassy area outside her house in Masefield Road. Both schemes charged a small fee and allowed the children to come and go as they pleased in sight of their own houses and in an open access basis.

The bouncy castle and parachute offered a different activity together with the ever popular bus play and face painting; the bus was certainly value for money.

The Adventure Playgrounds relied on the heavy mechanical Worthing bus to manoeuvre into its given location. At Langley Green Adventure Playground this proved very difficult and resulted in it breaking one of its windows on entry. Once on site the bus was an added attraction for each of the Adventure Playgrounds family days, it was paid to open on a casual basis for all the family visitors.

All in all with our promotional badges and T-shirts making our staff instantly recognisable, the scheme was a great success and following on from this, due to demand, we looked at helping set up a Parent and Toddler session in the district of Ifield Hyde Drive.

Although the playscheme did prove to be very successful it was felt with so much demand the association did overstretch itself. We were using the Bewbush Playbus for the airport sessions as well as the main playscheme; the Worthing bus was booked and used in Adventure Playgrounds as well as play centres. Although many of the sites had brought added awareness of our project and added support to our management committee it was felt that maybe our next scheme should look at focussing on fewer sites with perhaps more repeat visits.

Angela Flatt face painting on the Playbus play scheme at Broadfield

Parent & Toddler groups

Following on from our playschemes, Parent and Toddler groups were started. The first was located at Bewbush shops and the second at Ifield Hyde Drive. Both locations required the bus to drive and park in the local car parks and would encourage parents to drop in and share a chat and refreshments. Bewbush was run by two parent helpers: Annar Fazal and Julia Rigby. Julia was responsible for much of our publicity artwork as well as being involved in the beginning of the after school group.

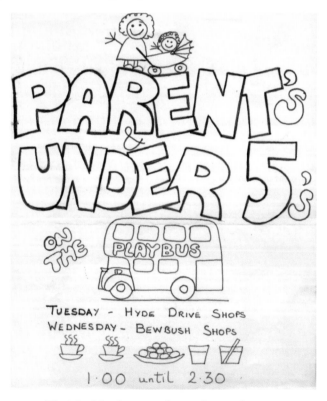

The Worthing bus was also used at Hyde Drive.

Children's parties

The Playbus raised further funds by providing the chance to use the facility for children's parties.

Some of the original parties were arranged by Philip Avery and his wife Val, who would not only deliver the bus but also hosted the party. The old bus had been better suited for static based parties beside the Leisure Centre.

This idea was started up again when the Association was trying to raise funds for the new bus. This time we could offer the vehicle without staff. Parents were given the chance to book the bus and to use it as they wanted. They would be charged a small fee for its use and would be responsible for the cleaning and safety of the vehicle.

The Worthing bus on location ready for use.

With the newer, more mobile Bewbush bus we were able to offer our service to different locations and it could park outside houses giving better access. Children could have the chance to use the full facilities provided, making a very different children's party. They could eat their food either on the bus itself or inside their own homes.

Users were advised and instructed on its safe use but then were left to undertake their own party session as they wished. The driver would deliver the bus to a given site and collect it for return at the end of the party after it had been cleaned. The option was to have the bus either on site at the Leisure Centre or at a chosen location.

This proved to be a popular and worthwhile way of increasing funding and saw the bus used often at quiet weekends. It further meant that the bus was not susceptible to attacks of vandalism at that time.

The Worthing bus was also available for use and was used in Brettingham Close, Bewbush. Parked outside with exit slide ready for use the children could play both inside and outside.

Worthing bus side view.

Inside the bus the children could use the facilities.

Group ready to enjoy their party food.

Group

National Playbus training rallies

London and South-East Region (LASER)

At the beginning of our new bus campaign in 1996 we realised that we had lapsed our membership with the National Playbus Association. We rejoined the association and began asking for advice and support on many issues. We were successful with grant applications as well as receiving advice and support. With this contact we were able to visit other local bus projects in Sussex to gain ideas not only on possible additional uses but also conversion layout.

We discovered that our pioneering project had once been a model example from which other projects had referred to.

The Newhaven bus was converted on an AEC Regent, the same as ours and their bus conversion was similar. Both the Worthing Buses and Sussex busses were on larger Leyland Atlantean models. Their groups included playschemes and Parent and Toddler groups. The Bognor project, was also an old style bus. All these projects were run similarly to us relying on volunteers and fund-raising.

Bognor bus seen at Tower Hamlets Rally.

Another bus we visited was the Brighton Playbus which was a statutory project operating in areas of deprivation in Brighton and worked mainly in after school and summer playscheme sessions. The Brighton bus could operate on a large scale with its paid workers working in and around Brighton using the large park areas in which to operate their groups safely. Most of all it was interesting to see the different uses and site locations for each project but it also relied on the belief and enthusiasm of its workers.

Through our re-forged links and contacts with National Playbus Association our project was able to keep up with changes in government legislation, which included, among others, changes in under fives legislation. This was as well as the proposed changes to EU driving regulations which could have marked the end for many voluntary projects as it was suggested that drivers should hold a PSV licence. This would prove not only costly to Playbus projects but also to many minivan community groups too. It was good to know that someone was researching and campaigning on our behalf.

As a precautionary measure NPA had secured 'Grandfather rights', for many drivers who had driven their vehicles for more than three years. These rights would ensure that projects could continue to operate without a PSV. Fortunately this measure was not necessary but it is still fun to be able to inform others that I am a 'Grandfather'!

We also learnt that NPA provided training events and rallies both regionally as well as nationally. In May 1990 the regional Rally was to be held nearby in Brighton at the Withdean Stadium. We saw this as a great opportunity to meet other projects and to see different mobiles from further afield than just Sussex itself. With our new red bus as our sleeping accommodation we were able to head off confidently.

This was the first event and the start of our new project. We were able to gain ideas on nature walks and games for use in our groups. We were also aware of the funding problems faced by other groups both voluntary and statutory as following this event and political changes both Lambeth and Hackney buses lost their funding overnight.

For the first time we were able to meet and talk with other workers who understood about chemical toilets, LPG gas fires, etc… didn't look at us oddly nor put us down for being different. We were able to talk frankly about our projects, gathering ideas for change and improvements. We were able to gain a wider idea and knowledge of our true worth and to see the potential of Working on Wheels.

We truly understood we were a mobile project which housed a playgroup. We slept overnight in our mobiles and chatted into the early morning. We realised a little too late we had missed a vital opportunity which could have helped us avoid some of our later problems as it was not always necessary to have a mobile to attend such an event. However, it did help locally and we were pleased to add our voice and support by attending further regional rallies.

We further became active members of the London and South-East Region (LASER) attending further training events and networking opportunities within the south-east.

Front view shot of Worthing and Bewbush.

Close up shot of the rear view of the Worthing and Playbuses.

Regional Rallies

1991 – Harlow

With our children in tow and sleeping overnight on the top deck of the Playbus we were able to attend workshops and learn ideas on such things as Circus skills, craft ideas, emergency and safety procedure as well as multi-cultural music. LASER had its own set of multi-cultural instruments which we were able to borrow ourselves and lend to other regional projects as well as use in local schools – these included the now infamous rainsticks.

Youth bus Harlow, with youth on the front!

Harlow black and white photograph. rest between training workshops.

Brigida Matthews and son Richie enjoying the well earned rest between training workshops.

1992 – Crawley (Hawth Theatre)

The London and South East Region 1992 Rally was hosted by Crawley at the Hawth Theatre.

We had at this time a parent involved who was a bus driver trainer and we were able to offer driver assessment sessions as one of our optional workshops. It was a proud moment for our project and despite not having to drive very far it meant that many of our workers could share the experience and training.

Leaflet designed by Julia Rigby.

1993 – Hounslow

We did not take our own bus this time but were allowed to stay overnight on another project bus. Learning face painting and circus skills helped us further.

1994 – Bognor

Sunny Bognor! As I was then teaching, our driver Geoff Riddick and Brighton worker Clive Parkinson drove down the night before having loaded the LASER multi-cultural instruments on board. They spent the night before playing with the wonderful rainsticks! Oh dear I had not warned them! The weekend was a thundery washout but despite this we were able to alter training and as ever the networking was much more valuable and a lot of fun.

1995 – Tower Hamlets (Docklands)

Tower Hamlets hosted this and the highlight was seeing the Albion Kids Show in full swing. It just showed that NPA was not just for double-decker buses but a mobile project could be any vehicle. The two trailers which they brought opened out to create a stage and a pirate boat. Albion Kids show participate more at events and their vehicles reflected this.

Some of the projects attending were able to show the public their vehicles including the inflatable exit slide.

The Albion trailer opens out to reveal the pirate boat.

Albion kids show van parks alongside our bus.

1996– Harlow

The LASER event was hosted at the outdoor pursuit centre in Harlow. We arrived late Friday night during which we were entertained by nature's own LASER display – a thunderstorm! Did I mention the rainsticks? But we did at least come up with an antidote by learning the 'sunclap' *. Our proposed workshops were changed and we were now offered rock climbing and abseiling. This proved not only a great team building experience but also enabled some of us to face our fear of heights. With Saturday afternoon canoe and kayaking sessions some of our members bravely attempted the seal run. A wet dunk for those brave enough to try. (Not me). As ever the networking and socialising made the event enjoyable and highly recommended. We even attended a kite making workshop and yes the kites really did fly. The idea was taken back and used in our after school group.

Afternoon kayaking on the river.

Seal run – Tina Murphy takes a dunk!

Tina Murphy after her trip down the canoe 'seal run'.

Team building on the rock wall.

1997 – Hackney (Hackney Marshes)

The weather added to the myth of the rainsticks. Yes the saga goes on. Hackney Playbus were returning the rainsticks and had moved them the Friday before the rally. We watched as the thunderstorm approached and torrential rain fell onto Hackney Marshes. But despite this it was a wonderful event and worth it to see yet another Albion Kids show trailer unfold. This time complete with musical theme. With upturned barrels, scaffolding poles, wheels and pipes it was wonderful to hear the sounds that eventually came tunefully out. Following this the rainsticks have been banned from rallies (and school events) although we do ensure the children know the sunclap too.

The Albion music trailer offers a chance for children to make a noise…

…and explore their musical talents.

National Rallies

National training events were scheduled to take place in September when most summer projects had come to the end of their busy summer work schedule.

After meeting many LASER projects in Brighton we looked forward to the National Playbus Rally 1990 which was to be held in Newcastle this year. With a newly painted bus we arraigned to travel for the event.

Both Geoff and I took our two children in the bus and headed up to Newcastle, while Angela Flatt with her three children flew up to Newcastle airport where they joined us. Between us we were able to attend many training workshops as well as meet projects from further afield than Sussex and London.

It took 10 hours to drive all the way to Newcastle from Crawley. It was the first time we had had a bus to take that was reliable and the experience of meeting other projects, seeing other bus's and sharing ideas was all worth it. Now we had a vehicle that could safely arrive at a destination without breaking down.

The climax of the training event in Newcastle was a convoy of projects driving through the city to Gateshead World International Flower Festival where the projects were offered to the public to view. A sight to behold and we were so pleased to have been involved.

In 1991 the rally was held much closer to home, at Brighton University. As with other events the option was to book a room or alternatively use the bus as a base. With the event being local we encouraged as many staff members as

1990 – Newcastle the buses park up safely.

Buses could be used for overnight accommodation.

The buses drove to the Gateshead flower festival.

Tower Hamlets Playbus.

possible to come along. It proved a valuable experience and opened the eyes of many project workers as they came to realise the bus was more that a playgroup.

Between 1990 and 2000 the Playbus attended many more rallies both National and Regional with or without our Playbus. We were able to compare project conversions and group working ideas and certainly should there have been a third Bewbush Playbus we would have had far better ideas to work with. We understood a little too late that it was not always necessary to take the bus along.

We were now confident members of both NPA and LASER and attended national events without the bus itself. We would arrange to meet and travel with other LASER members either on their projects or together on public transport. As ever the networking between members was important and valuable.

It was also good to be able to see the different types of equipment and resources that projects used and recommended especially as we needed to consider limited storage space. One of the earlier pieces of equipment we saw was the Fantasy Cube which was used continuously by the children at the Newcastle rally. A wonderful endorsement!

1991 – Brighton University we arrived and had a cup of tea.

National Rallies have also included:
   1992 – Coventry
   1993 – Manchester
   1994 – Swansea
   1995 – Nottingham

The Fantasy Cube in action!

1996 – Salford

1997 – Greenwich

1998 – Wakefield

1999 – Wakefield

2000 – Bristol

The Big Bus Bash in 2000 at Bristol was one of the last I was able to attend but I was fascinated at how many different projects were on show. The rock climbing wall which lifted from the top of the single Decker bus was a magnet of interest, as was the music tent which held scaffolding poles full of scrap materials where musical sounds could be produced. As ever, with the musical

Single decker bus with a rock climbing wall.

The rock wall lifted up, the bus stabilised and ready for action.

scrap which were made and added to from play work, the children began hitting hard and letting off steam but eventually settled to produce wonderful sounds.

From the different workshops we have attended we have been able to bring back and share many skills. These have included:

circus skills
multi-cultural music
nature trails
bus maintenance
emergency and safety procedures
equal opportunities
listening skills
drumming
face painting
arts and crafts
cooperative games
working in small spaces
signing
rock climbing
team building
kite flying
under fives legislation

But most important and valuable of all is the social networking and comparing project ideas. As well as the realisation that a Playbus is also not necessarily a converted bus but covers many other mobile facilities.

There is something about a mobile project which gets under your skin and inspires! It is the enthusiasm and belief which truly keeps many projects going. Although there are now far more different types of vehicles and different uses it is still those early playbuses which sparked the imagination!

The music tent held a variety of instruments made for scrap.

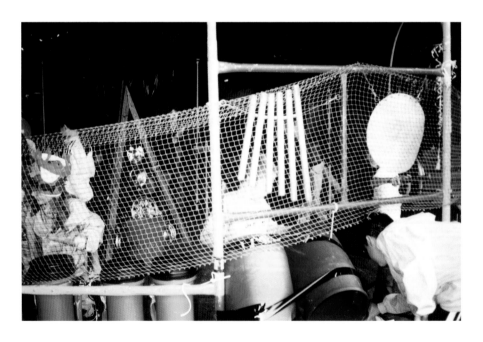

Bottles, hub caps, tubing – whatever could make a sound was used.

Initially children made a lot of lnoise but eventually they settled into making tuneful sounds; most importantly it was enjoyable.

Each project catered for a wide variety of clientele.

Networking and meeting with other workers.

Or, Seeing a wide variety of other projects. It was all worthwhile.

National Playbus Liverpool Victoria Challenge

Our project further became involved by becoming members of the NPA Board of directors. In January 1997 as part of the National Playbus Association, both Geoff and I attended the Liverpool Victoria Charity Challenge. The Charity challenge was set up by the members of the snooker community to use the popularity of Snooker to raise money for worthwhile causes. This year saw the 12 charities selected by the *TV Times*. The 12 charities were then allocated a world class player to play on their behalf.

Group proudly displays their signed 't' shirt.

This year National Playbus was lucky to be selected and was even luckier to have Steven Hendry MBE play on their behalf. The final was played on 5 January with Hendry playing Ronnie O'Sullivan, where Hendry had produced a fantastic finish to the Challenge in Birmingham by compiling a maximum break of 147 to complete the victory over Ronnie O'Sullivan.

Liverpool Victoria Challenge with Anthea Turner.

The victory earned the National Playbus Association a much needed £100,000. National Playbus had designed and produced their very distinctive red T-shirts with their logo especially for the event and seen by staff and volunteers on TV. At the end of the event both Ronnie O'Sullivan and Stephen Hendry signed one of the T-shirts for the Bewbush Playbus.

Group with 't' shirt.

The worst of times, the best of times

Bad times

Once our new bus had arrived we began to look towards the future. We had a project which could move off and serve others area and groups within the community yet the need for playgroup places remained the same.

With changes to the schools intake the playgroup became a younger age range. Our Playbus could not take children in under three so we were becoming limited in the service we could provide. We no longer had children who stayed for two years and without the older children the playgroup became younger in outlook too. We would need to begin to look at further developing our group work. The playgroup moved onto the new bus but there were problems which arose in the conversion and we started to look at using the old bus while further changes and improvements could be made. We also encountered major mechanical problems following an incident where children unkindly added gravel to our diesel tank. We did learn how to gravity feed the vehicle in order to reach our destination but we were facing replacing and installing new tanks. A little too late we added a lock to the diesel cap.

During one of our playschemes we had identified an area in Crawley Ifield Hyde Drive which had few facilities and we were asked to set up a Parent and Toddler group to support, this also led to us opening a second Parent and Toddler group at Bewbush shops. Both groups encouraged parents to come and meet with other parents as well as play alongside the children. Our staff provided refreshments and a chat as well as art and craft ideas. Parents in all groups were encouraged to take part in and support our committee with fund-raising.

Both groups would have to move onto the old bus temporarily to allow additional conversion work, but the Ifield group would probably have to close as now the old bus could really only operate from its static leisure centre site.

Sadly, before we could make any definite plans the old bus had been set alight and destroyed in an arson attack. Over the many years that the bus had been in operation we had come under attack before. We were unable to move the bus to a safe parking site due to reliability and to funding so we had to take our chances and leave the bus on site in Bewbush. The new interest that had been generated in the project had brought about further attacks of vandalism. Attacks had

The old bus was set alight and destroyed.

mainly been inconvenient and at worst a broken window or two but sadly in July 1991 our old bus had been destroyed. This time there was no chance of repairing the damage and the project was lost. Further with the planned re-conversion work we were looking at temporary closure of the project.

We were lucky to be able to sell the salvage to a bus enthusiast and the old bus was towed away the many miles to Dorset. It was a sad end to a much loved project and a much loved bus.

The fire had been started in the toilet area of the bus and had spread up through the bus. Although some of the equipment was salvageable the smoke damage meant that the cost of repair was not viable. With mechanically spare parts coming from museums this was seen as the right time to let it go. We had at least got our new bus in readiness and would have to hope group closures would only be temporary or short lived.

The cost of salvage was probably the same as the insurance value. The salvage company came and towed the bus away.

The bus ready to be towed away.

Ready to leave.

The bus was towed away.

The front driver's window was smashed after the fire.

Gone but with a host of memories the project still remained in our hearts.

Sadly, even when waiting for the bus to be taken away the vandals did not leave the bus alone and came back to break the front cab window.

Good times

In 1992 we were further contacted by the Worthing Playbus Association as their project was about to close its doors. We had recently met the project at the regional rally in Brighton. Sadly, just after this the Worthing Playbus Association had decided it could no longer carry on. It too had battled on with funding difficulties and the under fives changes in legislation and schools intake had seen their numbers drop. Their project had been far more mobile but difficulty in finding a driver/worker staff appointment had led them to think about calling it a day and closing their project.

The Worthing Playbus Association had heard of our plight and we were asked to come along to a meeting where it was decided that they would give us their Playbus in order to continue with our group work while conversion was under way.

As a voluntary project the Worthing Association could not profit by the sale and an agreement was drawn up.

Worthing Playbus Association
Contract of Sale

The 1968 Leyland Atlantean double Decker Bus Registration Number OCR 157G known as the 'Worthing Playbus' is hereby sold to the Bewbush Playbus association for the sum of £5 on the understanding that, should the Bewbush Playbus Association cease to operate the bus be sold, any proceeds be split with 50% of the proceeds being returned to the Worthing Playbus Association for the benefit of the children of Worthing.

Dated 19th March 1992

(Copy of contract of sale drawn up 17 March and signed for on the 19 March)

*The Worthing bus had a long fire exit slide which came from the top deck,
always a favourite.*

The bus was used for many years to help out in order to cover further conversion work; it was then given to another project in Newhaven, in return for a storage container to be parked beside the Leisure Centre.

It was sad to hear of their loss but was a welcome and much needed surprise for our project. It not only enabled groups to move onto their bus temporarily but it was a mobile vehicle which could still attend events as well as operate our groups.

It was even more special as on our visits around Sussex it was the Worthing bus which most caught our eye and seemed to be more in tune with ourselves. We loved their conversion especially the fire exit slide which came out from the top deck of the Playbus.

This slide was a popular attraction at school fairs where children could pay a small amount to go up and out the slide exit. This brought back memories of our old bus at earlier carnivals. As long as the exit was manned the children really loved the adventure stopping only to play briefly on occasion.

The after school group was the first to meet and greet the Worthing Playbus and loved the slide.

The after school club had spent much of their session in readiness for the Worthing Bus's arrival and had made flags and banners to welcome the new bus.

Now we were once more a two vehicle project and were able to keep open.

The Playgroup children were just as thrilled to see the Worthing bus.

After the loss of the old bus the Worthing and Bewbush bus were seen parked at the shops in Bewbush. The visual exterior of the project we saw as being very important in its promotion and effect.

Worthing and Bewbush bus seen parked at Bewbush shops car park.

The after school group with banners ready to welcome the Worthing bus.

The playgroup greeting their new bus.

Worthing and Bewbush bus seen parked at Bewbush shops car park.

The old and new playbus working at Gatwick Airport entertaining delayed passengers.

The Action Bus

By mid 1996 the Management committee of the Playbus decided that it would again be beneficial to carry out a further evaluation of existing services and future needs. Due to limited funding the evaluation was carried out by the association itself.

An annual report and business plan was drawn up which was published by CBC and funded by the community development unit.

The plan highlighted key areas for development. CBC also at this time came up with the funding for a part time worker, and Geoff Riddick, was appointed to the post.

Together with community development and the youth service the Playbus continued to endeavour to extend and develop both its services and its image.

In 2002 the Playbus livery was changed to reflect its new direction of work and to move away from the young image that the older livery portrayed. The Association also changed its name to Crawley Community Action Bus. The bus was beginning to move on to support youth and therefore the name was thought more appropriate. The bright cheerful young livery was changed to pink with logos in place.

Playbus now with CCAB livery pink.

Playgroup

The playgroup did continue to operate from the bus but the numbers had greatly reduced due to schools offering places for all four year olds. The group now catered for the under fours. Families now attended very briefly, which in turn reduced the voluntary support that could be offered from the parents. However, the group was still popular and it was decided to continue with the group as long as demand was there.

After School Club

The after school group continued to offer sessions for children in the First School with up to 25 children attending on a Thursday on a drop-in basis. The session offered children the opportunity to let off steam in a safe environment with sports, games and arts and craft activities each session.

However, with changes in the management of the First School, a failed OFSTED and changes with access to the playground the Playbus could no longer park safely in the school grounds. It did operate nearby for a time before moving off to work outside the Bewbush Leisure Centre's Youth Wing which was also near the children's playground.

Youth Action Broadfield

Youth Action Broadfield was a multi-agency organisation whose primary funders were the County Council, Borough Council and the Police Authority.

With the existing Broadfield Youth Centre closing for major modernisation, funding was secured from WSCC Youth Service and Youth Action Crawley. The action bus was funded to visit two sites in the neighbourhood, on Monday and Thursday evenings, for a period of ten weeks. Following initial suspicion and mistrust, the Action Bus was soon being used by separate groups of 15–20 young people at each site, and an occasional use by a group of 10–15 young people of Asian origin.

The attendance was far greater than when the youth centre had been open, and following positive evaluation by Jeanette Miller, the youth worker in charge, funding was continued for a total of ten months until the youth centre was reopened.

Bewbush and Broadfield Substance Misuse Programme

Funded by the Drugs Action Team, Drugs Prevention Initiative and Marks and Spencer, the Action bus was the base for three initiatives in the programme.

Young people designed a logo and title for publicity material used at a drug training event. The resulting logo and 'Don't be a Dope', title were then adopted by the WSCC Peer Education Project.

Initial designs for an 'anti drugs', spray painted mural were carried out on the Action Bus and was executed by the young people who attended. The resulting 30–40 foot mural was painted in Broadfield children's 'kick-about' play area.

'Calling All Parents' utilised the Action Bus on three daytime sessions giving parents the opportunity to talk and pick up information on controlled and legal drugs. Publicised through local schools and the local library the sessions were well attended.

In addition, Jeanette Miller came into Bewbush First School to undertake a series of PSHCE training workshops on smoking, drugs, and alcohol misuse; despite initial scepticism regarding the appropriateness of the subject it was agreed that whether we like it or not young children are aware of this and we should equip them to deal with the subject rather than sweep it aside.

Maidenbower Outreach youth work

Funded by WSCC – Youth development, the action bus was used for 12 sessions over six weeks to engage young people in the area and promote the opening of a new youth club. The sessions were attended by a large group of active 13/14 year olds, and visited by parents and other local residents. The Action bus evaluation showed that the proposed venue and opening time would not be ideally suited to the activities that the young people wanted. This

Town Square group.

led to WSCC youth service looking into opening a further session at a more suitable venue to cater for the needs of the group.

The Playbus now with strong links with the play service undertook a series of events promoting play. The bus was parked in the town centre square and was opened up to entertain passing children. With arts and crafts activities as well as face painting the bus proved once again a successful magnet and means of promotion.

Face painting arts and crafts.

With stilt walking clowns and promotional materials the bus could cope come rain or shine!

A further event was organised for the Christmas holidays and everyone was included and allowed to join in the fun.

Christmas group

Face painting in Town Square.

Welcare scheme

The Action bus continued to attend play scheme events as well as support Welcare in Horley where it was able to find a safe location for all its many visitors.

Parents drop-in Bewbush and Broadfield

The Community Development Unit at CBC approached the Action Bus to work in partnership with them to set up a drop-in for parents in Bewbush and Broadfield. The aim of the project was to set up and support groups in each neighbourhood using different approaches to attract local parents.

The Bewbush project started in late April 1998. Initially, the bus was used at a set location in the neighbourhood as an outreach facility to assess parents needs and inform them of the start of the project. Following this, the project moved into the local community centre where the staff continued to support the group and work with the parents and children.

The Broadfield project commenced in July 1998. It started in the local community centre. The Action Bus was then further used to undertake outreach work at six locations in the neighbourhood to inform the local parents of the group. The Action Bus was used as an attraction as well as advertising tool.

Staff from the bus were closely involved in these two projects. They worked with the children attending the drop-in providing quality childcare and ensuring safety. They were used to talk to parents, offering support and assessing their needs. The information was then used to shape the type of information sessions which could be provided for parents. In addition the staff provided general support in the running of the group.

'The bus provides a unique environment, both intimate and non-threatening. With its professional and friendly staff it is an invaluable community development tool. The bus has helped to make the parent support group very accessible and in no small way contributed to their success.'

(Mark Cozens, community development worker, Broadfield)

East Surrey Churches Welcare
Additionally the Playbus had been booked for a weekly drop-in session in Horley, Surrey, catering for homeless families in temporary accommodation. This was funded by East Surrey churches Welcare, who further funded playschemes during Easter and summer holidays over a number of years where the bus was supporting isolated and rural and communities including Tandridge and Mestham.

East Sussex Social Services further booked the bus to attend Heathfield, Uckfield and Crowborough offering play sessions.

As ever the scheme allowed the bus to drive and park at different venues.

Outside painting was always popular.

The bus could offload much of its outside play equipment.

Using every available green area.

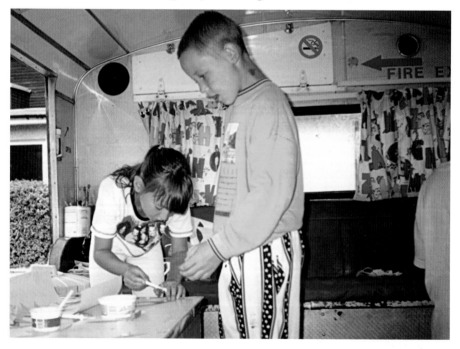

Inside, the bus craft projects were under way.

As well as the ever popular paint… *…or sand.*

The group was encouraged to use inside facilities.

175

Weather permitting the bus was more a focus than a necessity.

Surestart

The bus was use to offer initial creche and playscheme sessions for Surestart Broadfield including summer holidays prior to the construction of the main Surestart building.

The bus arrives and the children make their way.

A focus of attention.

Children were drawn to the scheme.

One of the last groups.

The Playbus finally closed its doors and ceased to operate in 2003. Sadly, rather than celebrating 25 years with the Queen's Golden Jubilee celebrations we mourned its loss and said goodbye.

The bus itself was now mechanically much more unreliable and not only difficult to maintain but difficult to service regularly. With no replacement on hand and not enough funding it was decided we should call it a day. The bus was given to the local Adventure Playground for their use.

Despite all the success and appreciation from all its users, the various groups had their own agendas and volunteers were difficult to find. With less focus on young children, parental support diminished and we had become a public service but without adequate funding.

With support from CBC our hopes were pinned on lottery funding, but this really was a grant application that had eluded us and had far too many hoops for us to jump through. Our management had become representatives with voices rather than our old hands-on root community supporters. The new bus from 1990 was now showing signs of age and wear. Perhaps in hindsight the association should have now sought a third vehicle to cater for the new direction in its client use.

Although the bus livery did offer a wider service, the bright appeal and love was no longer there.

Comic Relief

Over the years not only have we raised the funds for ourselves but helped other charitable causes including Comic Relief.

The first Comic Relief badges were designed in 1989. They were roughly made and we raised a £5 for comic relief. Two years later, in 1991, I tidied them up and added names on request. The teachers at the local Bewbush First School kept asking for more and more. Eventually, due to demand, on the Friday, we took the Playbus into the school playground and made badges on request. We made over £60 for comic relief. The badges then cost 30p.

It was decided that in return for the school's support that we would offer badge making at the school summer Fair and later the Christmas fair, raising money which paid for the badge making but also helping raise funds for others.

1993

The Splat Tomato. We copied the tomato from the Comic Relief Red nose design for the badges, it took lots of colouring! Geoff had to colour them all in, they were red with green stems. Geoff was having chemotherapy at the time so we were not sure if he was sick of colouring in or just sick!! The last one turned green and hence the tradition of one more. The Playbus crew had offered to come into the school to make the badges and went in dressed as clowns and made them with each class in turn.

1995

We liked these badges with their colour changing flowers. West Green joined in and wrote their own names and coloured their flowers. My last one came from there. I was working in Year 2 at the time and the class became involved in data collection as part of their maths work. We even had a granddad, who was a clown, who came in to school; he turned out to be Uncle Hughie!

1997

Licky lollies that turned your tongue red. We had gone back to boys and girls for this one but we also needed a badge for any we were not sure off. We also held a competition among the classes as to who would order the most. Mrs Jenn's class won the prize for the most badges ordered thanks to her daughter working at the council.

1999

This was the year of the colour changing noses! We used fluorescent pens for the noses around the side. We now not only had our Maths data collection but

also had links with the Post Office as well as Northgate School. My class learnt to sing *Wonderful World* with hand signs. We sang along with Alison Moyet which was a tradition we kept going in later years. In class we undertook a series of lessons which included the children in role play with blindfolds to experience visual disabilities.

2001

Pants to Poverty. The badge making event for Comic Relief had now become a tradition so it was decided that it would be a good idea to try and add the date to the design. We came up with boys and girls designs again, we may not have been too sure about the Pants T-shirt design but as ever we joined in the fun. This year we had all the classes join in on the day with Wellie throwing and other fund raising.

2003

This was a very tough year because the Playbus had finally closed and ceased to operate. In addition, Geoff Riddick, our main colouring in volunteer was very ill. However, with continued support from the school, as well as Northgate School, we decided to continue. We continued to collect data as well as offer badge making to the school.

2005

The two schools had now amalgamated and as I was now teaching in Reception my class undertook some simple counting activities as well as trips delivering badges in the main school using words such as over, under and through.

We went for a walk to the big school. We went to Year 5, through the doors, under the bars, across and along the corridor, around the corner, past some big children and over to the big school office. We had badges for the children.

And we sang *It's a Wonderful World*.

I had further supplied data, from the badge making, for any class higher up the school to use in whatever way they felt appropriate for their year group and to help make their learning real.

2007

Back to boys and girls with bows in their hair or bow ties. By now the amount of badges had been about 1,500 and the aim as ever was to try and reach 2,000. But we have never made it yet, despite the biannual support and tradition. The assembly this year included joke telling.

2009

My Year 2 class really enjoyed working out the maths problems every morning: coming in to work out the tally and the daily totals, as well as math problem solving. The theme was Doing something funny for the Money, I wasn't sure whether it should be a 'Haa! Haa! Haa!' a 'Hee! Hee Hee!' or a 'Ho! Ho! Ho!' but whatever, it was a laugh. The school had a celebration assembly with fashion show walk on the day itself. Singing *Help* and Doing Something funny for the money complete with video from Out of the Ark, it really was a lot of fun and laughter.

2011

This year having finally left Bewbush School I wondered if the badge making would continue. Although it no longer held or holds any links with the Playbus it is hoped funds this year will be put towards the book in its memory. The school was unable to join in this time but Northgate School once again rose cheerfully to the challenge, with Piratical names. So this year all the data information was handed to Northgate and in return I attended their summer fair with badge machine in tow!

It is hoped that the tradition will continue in some way in the future; perhaps not quite the bus itself but hopefully in memory we will keep it going.

Whatever happens, keep it going

Over the years the Playbus received a lot of support from its many users who gave their time and efforts voluntarily. Many of our original group users, now with young children of their own, look back with happy memories and wish their own children could experience the bus themselves. With fond memories the book will enable the project to carry on in some way.

The most important part of the Playbus was that it enabled and encouraged people to volunteer and get involved.

Crawley Museum

My mother, Mrs Elizabeth Wickstead, began helping the bus at the Pound Hill charity shop and would work every other Saturday raising over £600 to £1,000 a year. After its closure she continued to support other charities.

Now in her 80s she continues her work, this time for the Crawley Museum. As a family historian this is a subject close to her heart but it is also hoped this will further support the publication of the book from the museum. It is also hoped that the Silver Jubilee Plaque will be presented into the care of the museum.

NPA Three Peaks challenge

Our support and recognition for the role and potential of mobile work continues with Geoff Riddick currently Association manager of Working on Wheels.

Additionally my son and a group of friends decided to undertake the Three Peaks Charity Challenge. They chose to offer their support to the Working on Wheels National Charity and raised over £1,000.

Following the bus closure I had been contacted and asked to try and set up a new project or get the bus going again but unfortunately it all takes time and dedication. I really do believe mobile projects are important and valuable but

Three Peaks Challenge

Tom Riddick and friends.

like all voluntary projects they are a work of the heart and you need to take care of the heart!

Most successful projects rely on hard work and dedication as well as a love for the mobile, but in the end the funding is very important too.

Bewbush and Crawley were indeed very lucky to be part of this pioneering work even in they did lose it in the end.

The sun and the rain

The Bewbush Playbus staff and committee were, over the years, active members of both the NPA as well as the Regional group LASER.

We took charge and looked after the set of Multi-cultural instruments, adding to them as we could. This set comprised of traditional African drums; thumb pianos; bells; a Marimba as well as the now infamous rainsticks! The rainsticks really did seem to bring on the rain, not just rain but thunderstorms. It became a bit of a joke and so their story began.

We came up with our own version of the musical rainstorm during our summer playschemes.

To make a thunderstorm:

Start with finger clicks; then gently tap hands on thighs.

Tap louder and quicker, building up. Stamp feet on the ground quickly.

This proved great fun especially as the children took their turn to go downstairs on the lower deck of the Playbus to listen to the thunderstorm! It worked with the hollow floor in the school huts too.

However, the story of the rainsticks and their effects continued and the rainsticks were banned from events. But they still made such a wonderful sound.

So it was suggested we should learn the sun clap.

So we did.

It seems to work too!

Sun clap.

* The Sun Clap

. . . / . . - / . - - / - - - / - - . / - . . / . . .

[. = clap, / = pause, - = click fingers]

All aboard for a journey to the centre of the Earth
magazine article | Published in TES Newspaper on 5 March, 1999 |

By: Annie Bullen

Mobile classrooms can bring vital support to hard-pressed teachers or families. The National Playbus Association has been the driving force behind them for 30 years, reports Annie Bullen.

When a double-decker bus turns up at the school gates, it is not always time to go home. In Fife, Scotland, children climb on board for an exploration of their area's natural resources; in Birmingham, youngsters with learning difficulties play games to improve their maths and reading skills; in Crawley, Sussex, the arrival of the playbus signals after-school activities.

About 250 buses across the country have been converted to take specialist facilities into communities; half of these are school-based. The National Playbus Association, celebrating the thirtieth anniversary of the first playbus in Liverpool in 1969, helps to keep the buses running, funded by government grants, the National Lottery, donations and members' subscriptions.

"Although each bus is operated independently," says Lynne Williams, general manager at the association's headquarters in Bristol, "we provide practical help, from cheaper insurance and safety checks, through to training sessions and one-to-one advice."

The vehicles are not just buses to play on, however, they provide a wide range of educational services. They are particularly suited to providing back-up to facilities in schools.

The "MACbus" based run by Fife Council Community Services is based at the Kirkcaldy Museum and Arts Gallery. "Its real name is the Museum and

Arts Coach," says Emma Nicolson, the museum's outreach officer and former teacher, who says that demand for visits to primary schools far outstrips the four days a week the bus is available.

The current exhibition on "Riches of the Earth" digs deep to show why Fife looks as it does. It displays underground resources, such as minerals and potatoes and shows how they have influenced the local community.

Teacher's packs are sent out before the bus visit (which can last for three days) and the children are primed with quiz sheets. By the time they arrive, everyone is ready to examine the geology, agriculture, archaeology and natural history of the region. The children can see an earthworm farm, dig for garnets in volcanic sand, or study a display featuring the wool that comes from the sheep that eat the turnips that grow in the ground.

In Birmingham, the Saheli bus works closely with three primary schools in the Winson Green and Handsworth areas. Children with special educational or behavioural problems are referred to after-school sessions on the playbus. Teachers see it as a valuable resource where the children learn through play.

Mary Vadaie, a school governor and co-ordinator for the bus, is impressed with the amount children learn while they are on them: "They have been challenged to invent their own board games, which involve maths, English and interaction with other children."

The children often do not have English as a first language, so the seven playbus staff have been chosen for their range of languages: Punjabi, Urdu, Hindi, Gujarati and Mirpuri.

Mary Vadaie says the pre-school work is equally important, easing families into the school system and getting children used to sitting quietly, singing, or even using scissors. "Our children won't be the screamers when they start school," she says. "They've done the screaming with us - we've had the blood, sweat and tears."

Chris Smith, headteacher of Welford Road primary, one the schools that uses the Saheli bus, is unstinting in his praise for it. "We are fortunate to have it. The key factor is its mobility and our good working relationship with Mary and her team. They target particular groups who really benefit from the pre-school experience, while our home school partnership co-ordinator is able to identify children who can be helped by focused activities after school."

In Crawley, the playbus based at Bewbush primary is also used by after-school clubs, available as a drop-in for children who might otherwise be hanging around on street corners.

Geoff Riddick, who is this year's chairman of the NPA board of directors, is in charge. He is concerned that the recent emphasis on literacy and numeracy means other subjects are suffering: "Arts and crafts are being steadily squeezed out of the system," he says. "We do a lot of arts activities because many children have a talent which is not being nurtured. We have a hidden curriculum, if you like." The Crawley playbus scheme also offers after-school sports.

Geoff regards the Bewbush bus as a trailblazer, initiating projects that can then be handed on to schools. Sessions piloted in the bus for children with language and reading difficulties have been taken in to schools, and a project on substance-misuse, exploring drugs ranging from heroin and cocaine to nicotine and alcohol, has been taken into four local first and middle schools and other community groups.

Nationally, the majority of playbus schemes are run by volunteers who have identified a need in their community and every week 13,500 children somewhere climb on board.

Bewbush Playbus